W9-CJY-652

The American Cultural Dialogue
and Its Transmission

This book is dedicated to

DAVID P. BOYNTON

editor *extraordinaire*

in memory of nearly three decades
of collaboration and friendship

The American Cultural Dialogue and Its Transmission

George and Louise Spindler

with

Henry Trueba

and

Melvin D. Williams

The Falmer Press
(A member of the Taylor & Francis Group)
London • New York • Philadelphia

UK   The Falmer Press, Rankine Road, Basingstoke, Hampshire RG24 0PR

USA   The Falmer Press, Taylor & Francis Inc., 1900 Frost Road, Suite 101, Bristol, PA 19007

© G. D. Spindler, L. S. Spindler, 1990

All rights reserved. No part of this publication may be reproduced, stored in a retrieval system, or transmitted, in any form or by any means, electronic, mechanical, photocopying, recording, or otherwise, without permission in writing from the Publisher.

First published 1990

Reprinted 1992

British Library Cataloguing in Publication Data
Spindler, George
The American cultural dialogue and its transmission.
1. United States. Cultural processes
I. Title   II. Spindler, Louise
306.0973

ISBN 1-85000-773-X
ISBN 1-85000-774-8 pbk

Library of Congress Cataloging-in-Publication Data
Spindler, George Dearborn.
  The American cultural dialogue and its transmission/by George and Louise Spindler with Henry Trueba and Melvin D. Williams.
  Includes bibliographical references.
  ISBN 1-85000-773-X — ISBN 1-85000-774-8 (pbk.)
  1. United States — Civilization. 2. Intercultural education — United States. 3. Culture diffusion — United States. 4. Culture-Study and teaching — United States.
  I. Spindler, Louise S. II. Title.
  E169.1.S735   1990
  973—dc20

Jacket design by Benedict Evans

Typeset in 11/13 Garamond by
Chapterhouse, The Cloisters, Formby L37 3PX

Printed in Great Britain by Burgess Science Press, Basingstoke

Contents

List of Figures

Preface

This book has been written because we feel the need for it. We teach various courses such as 'Anthropological Perspectives on American Culture', 'Cultural Transmission', 'The Sociocultural Foundations of Education', that call for a book on American culture as a holistic process that does not get bogged down in the swamp of so much particularism, so much attention to static cultural norms, so much detail on various groups, classes, and regions that the whole gets lost. We have attempted to write such a book.

We have not tried to make *The American Cultural Dialogue* a comprehensive guide to the relevant literature. We have cited and referenced less than might be expected. We have provided some suggestions of useful reading and we have cited where we have had to, but by and large we have drawn from our own experience. That experience is long in time and broad in scope and includes more than three decades of data collection from university students. End notes at the end of chapters 1 through 8 and 11 refer to References found at the end of the book.

Many persons of linguistic and ethnic minority origin are full participants in the cultural mainstream and others aspire to this participation. Ethnicity does not disappear as a consequence of this participation. The cultural mainstream is in itself composed of ethnic groups and though White mainstream persons may become a minority in this country by the end of the twenty-first century, the cultural mainstream that has been so heavily influenced by them will probably dominate the cultural styles of the majority. Nevertheless, most minorities recognizable one hundred years ago in America are still recognizable and the United States has received a great stream of immigrants from dozens of countries during the past two decades. Ethnicity will not disappear from America.

The cultural mainstream is defined by the American cultural dialogue. This dialogue pivots around independence, freedom, conformity, success, community, optimism, cynicism, idealism, materialism, technology, nature, work and other value orientations and their permutations and oppositions. The dialogue goes on and has gone on since the Revolution. Immigrants and those rising from lower socioeconomic ranks assimilate, appropriate and acquire this dialogue as they become mainstream. This assimilative process will go on, for it is the American ethos, the central process of American culture and society. Ethnicity is not lost but participation is gained. However, ethnicity is reshaped.

We claim to be multicultural, diverse, and proud of it, but cultural assimilation has taken place in America and it is taking place today. The struggle for ethnic identity and recognition has quickened. Talk of 'assimilation' is now unpopular in education, the social sciences, and politicians seeking minority votes. And yet it is occurring as a necessary corollary to full participation . . . to success in America. The balancing of assimilation and preservation of identity is constant and full of conflict. This is part of the American dialogue and it has always been a part of this dialogue. It is the nature of cultural dialogues that they rationalize, deny, defend, protest and exhibit.

What we have written in this book is not adequate to the task we have set for ourselves. It is not adequate as a representation of the complexity of the American scene and the currents of dialogue enlivening it. Our writings express a way of looking at ourselves rather than a finished analysis of what we are and can become.

Realizing our own limitations we have invited Henry Trueba and Melvin Williams to write separate chapters on the experiences of their own ethnic groups as part of the dialogue. Their chapters afford different and fresh perspectives on some of the same processes of adaptation, reaction and change that we discuss in the main text. They would have written a different book than we did but they have graciously consented to participate in this one. Their experience and perspectives are indispensable.

About the Authors and Contributors

George and Louise Spindler started doing field research as anthropologists in America in 1948 and have continued ever since. They have observed the Menominee and other Native American communities, researched in West Coast schools, and in schools in the Mid-west, and have lived and researched in several Mid-western as well as California communities. They have also done extensive field research in Germany.

The Spindlers have traveled by car on the back-roads and byways in every state of the Union excepting Hawaii. They have crossed from California to Wisconsin and back eighty-seven times, from and to both coasts eight times, and camped along the way or stayed in 'ma and pa' motels and hotels in small towns. They have talked to hundreds of people in small towns, villages, and cities. They have observed and conversed with the trained eyes and ears of the cultural anthropologist.

We feel that it is important for both authors and readers to be aware of their sociocultural origins in the context of this kind of book. We try to rise above our biases but it always helps to understand what they might be.

George Spindler's maternal side is pre-Revolutionary, when Phillip de La Noye (later Delano) came over to Plymouth on the good ship *Fortune* in 1621. His paternal side, also pre-Revolutionary, landed in Baltimore, Maryland, in 1760, from Amsterdam, and then moved to Pennsylvania and finally to Ohio, where his father, Frank Nicholas Spindler, was born. Frank Spindler was Professor of Psychology and Philosophy at what is now the University of Wisconsin at Stevens Point until his death in 1935. Louise Spindler's maternal side came from Norway in mid-nineteenth century and her father's from Alsace-Lorraine at about the same time. They both grew up in upper-middle class professional/business families, George in the Mid-west, Louise on the West Coast.

George received his Ph.D. in cultural anthropology with fields in psychology and sociology at the University of California at Los Angeles in 1952, and his M.S. in the same fields at the University of Wisconsin at Madison in 1948. Louise was the first Ph.D in anthropology at Stanford and of course the first woman to receive the degree there (in 1956). George has taught at Stanford since 1950 in a joint appointment in anthropology and education, with appointments as visiting professor at the University of Wisconsin at Madison and the University of California at Santa Barbara. They have published extensively in the psychology of culture change and modernization, the ethnography of education, cross-cultural sex roles, American culture, and the comparative analysis of schooling in Germany and the United States.

Henry T. Trueba was born in Mexico City from parents whose Basque families came from the Navara Province at the turn of the century. He entered the Jesuit Order in 1947, in which he remained until 1965. He arrived in Maryland in 1961 to complete his theological studies and subsequently obtained his M.A. in Anthropology from Stanford, and his Ph.D. in Anthropology from the University of Pittsburgh. His earlier work as a missionary among the Mayas, as well as his field work research with linguistic minorities in this country during the 1960s and 1970s have been the center of his intellectual work and a crucial factor in his understanding of American social, institutions and cultural values.

He has travelled through Europe, Micronesia and Latin America, and has worked in different states and universities dealing with educational equity issues, first and second language acquisition issues, minority academic achievement, cognitive development and mainstreaming.

Melvin D. Williams is professor of anthropology and director of the Comprehensive Studies Program at the University of Michigan. Before that he taught at Purdue University and was director of its African Studies and Research Center. He held the Olive B. O'Connor Chair in American Institutions at Colgate University in 1976–1977. He was chairman of the Department of Sociology and Anthropology at Carlow College from 1973–1976. Dr. Williams was an associate professor of anthropology in the Department of Anthropology at the University of Pittsburgh from 1976–1979. He is author of numerous articles in professional journals and of books including *Community in a Black Pentecostal Church*, *On the Street Where I Lived*, and editor of *Readings in Afro-American Anthropology*. He was active in community affairs in Pittsburgh, where he was born and educated.

Acknowledgments

Many people have read drafts of this book. To name any of the students who have read parts of the whole, or the whole, would be unfair, since all contributed insight and knowledge. We will name certain colleagues who have contributed greatly to our understanding of what we are trying to do. Ray McDermott encouraged and criticized. As he said, 'You have written a book about America that is not what I would have written but it is worth knowing your America.' Sandy Robertson reacted so violently to some chapters that he spilled coffee on them but nevertheless produced telling criticisms and challenges and thought the book should be published. (Since he is a British anthropologist he doesn't believe in culture anyhow.) Mariko Fujita and Toshiyuki Sano, Japanese anthropologists who have studied America on their own, questioned our concept of dialogue and suggested other ways of handling the material, but said that if we published the book, they would use it in their teaching about America. Henry Trueba provided thoughtful encouragement and criticism from the beginning and to him we owe a special debt. Spring quarters as visiting professors at the University of California, Santa Barbara, in the Cross-Cultural Program administered by him in the School of Education, kept us in close contact during the book's formative states. We are also grateful to the Department of Anthropology at UCSB, for support, friendship, and input. To the Department of Anthropology and School of Education at Stanford we are grateful for the many years of freedom to develop ideas and experiment with ways of teaching them to both graduate and undergraduate students.

And to Louise Bay Waters, a graduate student in the School of Education at Stanford in the mid-seventies, we owe a special debt, since it was her paper, *The Ethnicity of White Non-Ethnics*, that stimulated us to pursue certain interpretations of relations between minorities and the mainstream in America; to Beatriz Jamaica for word-processing several drafts of this writing; to Betsy Lancefield who searched census tracts for relevant demographic data and prepared diagrams expressing these relevances; to Hector Mendez, who prepared others; to Nannette Daugherty, who put the finishing touches on the formatting of the manuscript; and to Carol Saumarez and Kate Miller, respectively editor and copy editor at Falmer Press, we are grateful for indispensable help.

George and Louise Spindler
Stanford University

Chapter 1

Introduction

This book is about the culture of the United States of America from an anthropological perspective. Many interpreters of America feel that there are too many subgroups, too many varieties of opinion and lifestyles, too few common interests and experiences, and too little history in common for there to be any 'American' culture. In one sense this is bound to be true given the obvious diversity within the American scene. But still, we manage somehow to communicate with each other even if we are often in conflict. We have pursued common goals during historical periods that have become a part of our past and we strive for some common causes today. We have a creed which is often stated and often flouted — that we are all equal and that no one shall be disadvantaged by their race, creed, or color. We have great documents such as the Declaration of Independence and the American Constitution which lay out in detail many of our ideals.

Perhaps what we have in common is a way of talking to each other about our common interests and our differences. We may express our commonalities as clearly in the framework of conflict as we do within the framework of cooperation. We are in a constant dialogue that can be construed as a *cultural* dialogue. This dialogue has been going on for some time and about some of the same things, such as individual achievement and community, equality, conformity and difference, honesty and expediency, and success and failure.

We define *cultural dialogue* as culturally phrased expressions of meaning referent to pivotal concerns such as those just mentioned. These concerns are phrased as 'value orientations' but the dialogue expresses *oppositions* as well as agreements. The expressions occur in public speech and behavior, in editorials, campaign speeches, classrooms, the mass media, churches and religious ideology, and so forth. They occur in private speech and behavior as people accommodate and conflict with each other as spouses, friends, partners, parents and children. The pivotal concerns and the agreements and conflicts centered around them are both *in* individuals and *between* persons as social actors in the situations provided them by their society. We have chosen to focus on only certain areas of the American cultural dialogue and much of the data on which our analysis is based has been elicited from college students, though we have drawn from our own experience in America, and that of others, as well.

This book is therefore about the American cultural dialogue rather than simply about American culture. The term 'American culture' implies a fixed, static, set of expectations, values, ways of thinking, and ways of behaving. Such a concept of culture does not even always work well for a relatively isolated, self-contained human community. We think of 'culture' as a *process*. It is what happens as people try to make sense of their own lives and sense of the behavior of other people with whom they have to deal. Cultural understandings make communication possible. Many of these understandings are understandings of difference.

To discuss further what culture or cultural dialogue is or is not would be futile at this point. Instead, it seems appropriate to anticipate what we think a book about the American cultural dialogue from an anthropological perspective should be about.

Themes

We propose that there are certain aspects of the American dialogue that have considerable continuity through the last 200 years or so. They emerged before the Revolutionary War and they have continued in changing but recognizable form through to the present. Identifying some of the most important promontories of that continuity will be one of our purposes.

At the same time it is clear that though there has been demonstrable continuity in the American process there is also change. In fact the dynamism of change, particularly technological change, is sometimes considered to be the dominant feature of an American culture. Americans are said to value change. 'A new broom sweeps clean' was a meaningful political slogan in the early twentieth century. Americans seem to have great faith that advances in technology will solve basic problems — some of which threaten our existence. We predicate our lives upon the notion that change will occur and that on the whole it will be for the better. Americans are said to be optimistic and future-orientated but even this orientation towards the future is undergoing change.

Conflict and diversity often seem more apparent than continuity. The American population is composed now of more than forty ethnic groups and a very wide diversity of religious identifications. There is also the diversity of small and large political, social and religious movements, regional diversity, social class diversity, and ideological diversity. Difference can always be a source of conflict and the American scene is full of conflict. And yet somehow this conflict does not result in the upheavals that have occurred elsewhere in the world. When Richard Nixon resigned the presidency on August 9, 1974, an event that certainly would have shaken most societies to the core, most of us hardly noticed the difference. The student riots and occupations of university buildings in the 1960s and 1970s did not threaten the continuity of our society or its government, nor did our ruling bodies react by killing hundreds of students. At times we actually seem to enjoy conflict and value diversity. At other times conflict and diversity are expressed in highly destructive terms. Nevertheless we manage a surprisingly high degree of communication in the midst of great diversity and wide-ranging conflict.

There is implied in our kind of diversity a working accommodation to it. Small groups of people in America, with some notable exceptions, do not seem to want to obliterate each other. After the election is over most of us accept the dictum of the people. We seem to expect youth to be deviant and express their deviance in hairstyles, costumes, music, and social behaviors that are in some degree irritating or challenging to adults. Yet we do very little about trying to eliminate those behaviors or to make youth conform. Foreign observers are amazed and intrigued by the diversity of the American scene and, despite our reputation as a violent society, our apparent tolerance for any difference that does not affect us personally.

All cultures must be transmitted to new generations if they are to survive. The American cultural dialogue is expressed in manifold forms, in the rhetoric of politics, in editorial diatribes, in the mass media, in advertising, in the symbols of wealth, power, poverty and dissidence. Our schools are an arena for our cultural dialogue and we will be particularly concerned with them and with how change, continuity, diversity, conflict, and accommodation are orchestrated in them.

These basic themes will be present in some form in our analysis of all of the topics we cover in this book. We can mention those topics now, with the understanding that we are merely pointing in the various directions we expect to go rather than providing a blueprint for exactly how things will work out.

Ethnic and Social Class Composition of American Society

Our first task will be to try to achieve some understanding of the ethnic and social diversity of American society. This is not easy to do because this composition is constantly changing and the labels that are used for census data do not always allow a very close approximation of the kind of reality in which we are interested. Nevertheless there are some things that we can say that will provide a backdrop for analysis of the American processes of cultural continuity, change, conflict and accommodation.

Core Mainstream Culture

The term 'mainstream' is used widely but carelessly. Who is mainstream? When we use this term are we talking about White Anglo-Saxon Protestants, or are we talking about people, irrespective of ethnic origins who practice in their daily lives some common cultural features? Are there subdivisions of the mainstream that are important? We are going to present some interpretations with which not everyone will agree. We will maintain that there are some core values that have been a part of the American dialogue since the beginning and that these have been carried on within a mainstream construction of American culture. We are also going to hypothesize that there is a subset of the mainstream that can be referred to as a referent ethni-class. This ethni-class, we propose, has historical roots and in fact has acquired its referent status due to this historical continuity.

Education as Cultural Transmission

The way any culture maintains itself is through education and the American culture is no exception. The problem is *what* culture is to be maintained? A look at our schools as they have been historically formed in America suggest that there is a high degree of mainstream conformity and historicity. The major function of education has been described by many analysts of the American scene as the major instrument of the 'melting pot'. The melting pot idea itself has become very suspect. Americans of different persuasions and ethnicities object to being 'melted down' to a conglomerate mass. What is surprising, however, about American society is that so many people do begin to act in predictable 'American' ways and acquire the instrumentalities for economic, social, political, and personal survival in our complex society. The schools are by no means altogether accountable and yet they *have* had an influence. Our analysis will be directed at what this influence is and how it has been accomplished.

The school in America has been accused of being mainly an instrument of the mainstream middle class. We will attempt to see what this can mean and whether this orientation is accountable for the trouble in the schools.

Are our schools so heavily culturally loaded with mainstream values that many ethnic groups and social classes find themselves in opposition to the culture promoted in them? Are there ways that we could bring more of the diverse elements of our society into a productive relationship with our economic and social institutions? Why are about 25 per cent of our youth dropping out of school before they acquire a high school diploma? Have we somehow decided to throw away one-fourth of our coming generation? Are our schools designed for failure as much as for success?

Diversity

The notion of diversity keeps coming up in our discussion and will be a very important theme. We have already said that we will try to define that diversity and we have hinted at some of the conflict relationships between diverse elements. One of our major themes will be the conflicts and accommodations that occur between certain mainstream cultural elements and groups and nonmainstream elements and groups, or diversity and opposition. It is possible to think of American society as composed almost entirely of diverse groups in conflict with some hypothetical mainstream culture. If we define the mainstream population as White Anglo-Saxon Protestant and male-dominated, then most groups, including women and children as well as all ethnic groups that are not White Anglo-Saxon Protestant and male, are in some degree of diverse opposition to this mainstream culture. This is possibly carrying the matter too far but for the sake of argument we will present some support for this model of American society.

One particular element of American society that is usually left out of discussions of American culture is the Native American population. These were the people who were here before the rest of us came. They had well established and also very diverse cultures. There were at least some 375 different languages spoken in North America before the Europeans came and this linguistic diversity was matched by social and cultural diversity. Between most of these cultures and the Euro-American culture that developed there were virtually unresolvable conflicts — political, economic, social, ideological, and cultural. In some ways the Native American conflicts and accommodations to the mainstream are an exemplification of the conflicts experienced by other diverse elements and the mainstream. We will therefore spend some time on this complex set of articulations and disarticulations.

We also forget easily that one of the major differences between American culture and European culture is the influence of Native American cultures upon the developing Euro-American society and culture. For example, some of the most distinctive elements of the American vocabulary are words derived from American Indian languages. A major part of our food supply comes from plants domesticated by American Indians (and corn is practically a national vegetable). Some of our concepts of masculinity, of the frontier, and a minority view of our relationship with nature, are heavily influenced by Native American conceptions. Black and Hispanic, as well as Asian influences on the making of America have been profound as well. We have recognized this by inviting Henry Trueba and Melvin Williams to write chapters on the Chicano and Black experience within the American cultural dialogue.

Hinterland Culture

In most treatments of American relationships the country as a whole is cast as though it were one big urban conglomerate or, historically, one vast rural society. We are going to develop a concept that we will term the 'hinterland'. This is a concept that is not exactly coterminous with 'rural'. There are hinterlanders living in the city, and there are many urbanites living in the country. The hinterland does tend to be more rural than urban and in one sense it can be thought of as those vast areas between our great metropolitan centers peopled by individuals who are there for a number of reasons, not the least of which is to escape the city. There has always been an intermigration between the city and the country in America, though most often in favor of the city. But recently there has been a sizeable migration of city dwellers to the country. What are they looking for? Are there hinterland values, ideologies, expectations, that are not only different from those most common in the city but in partial opposition to them? Do hippies and 'hillbillies' have something in common? Do yuppies and street people, particularly drug hustlers, have something in common? And what about the stubborn people for whom farming is not merely a way of life but for whom farming is life itself? Are there hard-pressed small town values that people try hard to maintain in the face of a flood of alternative views promoted by the mass media?

Movements in American Society

Movement is the keynote of American culture, but here we are thinking of socio-religious movements. Many of the most recent movements have been fundamentalist in character. Some commentators seem to think that fundamentalism is new in America. On the contrary, fundamentalism is partly what American culture has been historically about. Many of the people who came to America, such as the Puritans, were fundamentalists. Whenever America has been in trouble fundamentalism has become rampant. We cannot possibly look at all of the dozens of the fundamentalist movements that have appeared so suddenly and so dynamically over the past twenty years or so but we will examine one or two of them. As we do so we will see that there is not so much deviation from some core values in American culture as one might think.

Future Shock

A special subset of the theme of cultural change has been made popular by a film titled *'Future Shock'* narrated by Orson Welles and derived from the book by Alvin Toffler of the same title. An examination of this film is instructive. Though it was cast in the mold of the late 1960s and early 1970s, it is valuable as a way of entering the American cultural dialogue. If one looks at it as a part of the dialogue and not necessarily an accurate forecast of the future, or even of the problems related to the future and to change, it can be very useful. In this film and in much of the American dialogue about change and the future since World War II there are certain concepts that appear and reappear. The 'age of anxiety', 'overchoice', 'prepackaged and plastic', 'accelerated pace of change', 'nothing is permanent anymore', 'the move', 'loss of the sense of belonging', 'all relationships are temporary', and 'the death of permanence', these phrases and the images they evoke have become a part of our cultural self-concept.

The film shows dramatically and effectively changes that were occurring at the time the film was made and anticipates future changes. Since we have already arrived in a part of the film's future, we have some perspective that was not available when the film itself was made in 1972. The future with humanoids serving us behind the counter of an airport, the installation of temporary body parts, the development of artificial intelligence, genetic engineering, a genetic race, is partly already here. A tired man gets up in the morning and plugs himself in for a little shock to get going. He plugs his female partner in to get her up as well. There is marriage between homosexuals. There are young people sleeping together on the beach for a one night stand. Computers seem to run everything.

The images center upon and communicate a sense of anxiety about choice and impermanence. The film and the questions it raises and the images it provides are worth considering because they are not entirely illusory. It is apparent that we are in the midst of rapid technological and social change and that the former sources of security in presumed stable family relationships and communities are threatened.

The question, however, is whether or not this sense of crisis and the anxiety about change and the loss of permanence are really very new on the American scene. When the westward movement was taking place there was little permanence for the people who made the move. The westward movement was in turn preceded by the migration of peoples from the old world to the new, and for them there was little permanence during the process of migration and adaptation. It may be that the permanence that the film and many discussions of this kind seem to assume we once had is an illusion. When Lloyd Warner went to study a 'Yankee city' he wrote as though he were dealing with established, permanent, 'old American' communities. A careful examination of the populations that he was actually working with makes it clear that he was not dealing with permanence but rather with a culture form that had been quickly adapted by newcomers.

We think of small towns in America as being filled with people who have been there for generations. There is very little in census data to indicate that that is true. In small towns of under 30,000 people, in the Mid-west, more than half of the population is of very short tenure, under ten years. There has always been change and impermanence in American society.

Our attitude towards change and particularly technological change and its consequences is one of deep ambivalence. Americans look upon change as essentially desirable: 'You can't stop progress'. But at the same time we decry the upsetting results of radical technological change. We want some things to stay the same at the same time that we want improvement, progress, and development. Or we may think that we don't have enough technological change rather than too much. The problems of toxic waste, pollution of the atmosphere, the 'greenhouse effect', the deterioration of the Van Allen ozone belt, the paving over of fertile farmland that could be used to produce food rather than support new developments — all of these changes can presumably be ameliorated or their direction changed by a yet more advanced technology that lies in our immediate future.

Our attitude towards change and the reality of technological change seems to be accountable for the increasing attempts by Americans to return to an illusory permanence and security of the past. We have some evidence, that we will use later, that there has been a cycling of value orientations in the dialogue of American culture since World War II and that we are now, in 1990, in a currently rather fundamentalist and tradition-orientated phase of the cycle. Part of the dynamism of American culture seems to be created by the relationship between change, attitudes towards change, and the psychological consequences for individuals.

Americans, for example, are a very transient people. In the California schools where we have worked, more than half of the children in the elementary school have not resided in the school district for more than one year. Indeed, many have lived there for less than one year. Americans are constantly on the move. This is a major theme of the film *Future Shock*. Promotions, occupational changes, sometimes changes in fortune, dictate that the family pull up whatever roots it has put down and move once again to a new town and a new neighborhood. Much has been written about the trauma of such separations from one's community, particularly for children whose peer relationships are disturbed. These moves may not be as upsetting as they are sometimes portrayed, however, because Americans are able to replace friends, neighborhood networks, peer groups, and even, to some extent, identities when they arrive in a new community. The principle of 'replaceable parts' seems to be operating. If one moves into a new neighborhood very much like the old one, into a suburb of about the same status as the old one — perhaps even a little better — one finds the same kinds of people there. If children and youth go to about the same kinds of schools, drawing from about the same kinds of school districts as the ones that they left, they too will find friends quite similar to the ones they left behind, although sometimes it is more difficult for children than adults.

This transient quality of life does, however, have some consequences. One's commitments to other people are unlikely to be maintained at a deep level under these circumstances. If friendships can be replaced, then friendship may not mean as much as it did, or at least could. One's own identity can be marred by the casual attitudes of others and the lack of truly intimate relationships. We would expect also that one's interest in the maintenance of the community would shrink and there would be a tendency for more emphasis on one's own self-interest since no community is even semipermanent. The eternally transient quality of American life may therefore result in a kind of marginalization which is reflected in one's relationships with virtually all social institutions, groups, other individuals, and perhaps even work.

Some young people have opted for rural communes, a return to the farm, and, less dramatically, a refusal to move for purposes of promotion. Where it was unheard of a few years ago for an individual, particularly a male 'breadwinner', to refuse a promotion that would entail moving the family, today this is not so uncommon. Sometimes flexible arrangements in breadwinning make it possible for a shift in responsibilities both domestic and economic to occur, that will allow the family to stay in one place for longer time — sometimes long enough to permit the children to grow up. This is very hard to support except with anecdotal evidence. In any event, the transient quality of American life seems to be a permanent feature of our times and one to which we all have to adapt.

In Prospect

No one book or any one author or group of authors can possibly reduce the complexity of American culture to a single, systematic, simplified statement. We can only select for examination certain aspects of the dynamic relationships that constitute our ongoing culture. We have tried to simplify matters by focusing on the American dialogue, but many excursions will be made into other areas and relationships. These might not be the same things that other analysts would choose.

Notes

This chapter opens many topics that will be considered and annotated later. For now we refer to H. Trueba, G. and L. Spindler, Eds. (1989), *What do Anthropologists Have to Say About Dropouts?* A. J. Hallowell (1957) on the influence of American Indian cultures in American culture. Alvin Toffler (1970) *Future Shock* and the film by that title, and Lloyd Warner (1941). All references cited are listed under *References*, p. 171 ff.

Chapter 2

The Composition of American Society

Who is 'Ethnic' or 'Minority'?

Each year that we give our course 'Anthropological Perspectives on American Culture' we administer a 'pretest'. This pretest asks students on the first day of class to answer the following questions:

1. Is there an American culture? If the answer is 'yes' describe it briefly.
2. Are you a member of a minority group? Yes or no. What is a minority group?
3. Are you a member of an ethnic group? Yes or no. What is an ethnic group?
4. What core values of American culture do you feel that you personally hold?
5. Name eight minority groups currently in the United States.

The responses to this pretest will be described in this and the next chapter as we analyze the cultural distribution of characteristics in American society. For this chapter what is most relevant is the identification of respondents with minority status and their comprehension of minority groups in the United States.

About half of the respondents to question two indicate that they are not members of minority groups while the other half indicate that they are. This seems straightforward enough except that when when one examines the relationship between this response and presumed minority group membership the correlation is by no means perfect. About 25 per cent of those who indicate that they are members of minority groups are not, if we define mainstream as being Caucasian and native English speaking as many respondents do. Some Caucasian, native English speaking respondents regard that designation in itself as a designation of minority status. On the other hand, about one-third of students who would be defined as members of minority groups in that they are not Caucasian and native English speakers do not define themselves as minorities but rather as members of the mainstream group. Their definition of themselves is based upon their behavior — their attitudes and values — in short, their culture. For them, questions of ethnic origin and particularly of race are not relevant.

Most respondents define a minority group as being a group that is smaller than the majority or mainstream and that is different in some way. The differences are usually described as language, beliefs, values, or specific cultural traits not held by the majority. Some respondents refer to a 'racial' factor of difference.

In response to the question three, about 40 per cent of the respondents indicate that they are not members of an ethnic group and about 60 per cent indicate that they are. An ethnic group is defined as a group with a sense of identity, a strong common bond, a common heritage, values, beliefs, and history, that is different from the majority or mainstream. They are often seen as from 'another country'. The tendency that we noted for these distinctions to be blurred with the responses concerning minority group status hold here as well. A number of respondents who are Caucasian and native speakers of English, regard themselves as members of an ethnic group, such as Irish Catholic or even Irish Protestant, Moravian, Armenian, Italian, or Polish. Most of the respondents in categories of this kind, however, do not define themselves as members of ethnic groups but as part of the 'mainstream'. This applies even to some individuals whose ethnicity seems apparent to others such as Asiatics, Hispanics, and Blacks but who identify themselves as 'mainstreamers' and feel that their ethnic 'identity' is not particularly important.

Respondents name a number of minority groups in response to question five. A partial list includes Blacks, Mexicans, Chinese, Japanese, Native Americans, Vietnamese, Iranians, Jews, Cubans, Indians (from India), Armenians, Moravians, Haitians, Puerto Ricans, Cambodians, Irish, Italians, Mormons, and farmers, the homeless, the jobless, and the PTL (Praise the Lord) Club. An increasing number of respondents also list 'women' as a minority group.

What the responses to this pretest show us is that the terms 'mainstream', 'minority group', and 'ethnic group', are not as precisely defined as some of our national dialogue would suggest. It is often apparently assumed in the mass media, in discussion of public policy, and even in education-related analyses, that these terms are understood by everyone in about the same way. The rest of this chapter will be devoted to an attempt to give these concepts further definition so that we will have a more coherent view of the composition of American society in the USA.

A Problem of Definition

Our problem, then, is to define more precisely the meaning of terms such as 'mainstream', 'minority group', and 'ethnic group'. We will do this by providing information on the distribution of various groups in American society. We will use proportionate terms in recognition of the fact that our population is changing rapidly both in absolute size and in the relative distribution of groups in relationship to each other. The materials that we are presenting are based upon the 1970 and 1980 censuses corrected where possible with more current information.

Figure 2.1, 'American Ethnicity', shows us the complexity of American society in terms of three major variables — ethnicity, nationality, and religion. Socioeconomic status and social class are left out for the sake of simplicity. These dimensions may be of more importance than any of the others in the emerging American society and we will come back to them later.

This chart itemizes twenty-four groups named by national origin, which are categorized into six major named ethnic categories and further subdivided by five major religious categories. The interaction of these variables can produce a profile of even greater complexity since any of the categories may combine in ways not indicated in the chart and, indeed, the 'other' categories can be further subdivided into named groups. Any Asiatic individual or group, for example, may be Buddhist, Protestant, or 'other' including Catholic or membership in any of the several dozen small religious movements or sects.

Two headings in the row extending from the category 'ethnicity' need further explanation. European 'non-ethnic' versus European 'ethnic' cannot be thought of as scientific categories but rather as reflecting folk definitions of ethnicity. European 'non-ethnic' is broadly equivalent to 'mainstream' in the thinking of most people. In fact the mainstream is often defined as Anglo-Saxon, North European, and Protestant. A little over half of the total American population does belong to this category. Historically, in American communities, Catholics of European origin have been regarded as members of ethnic groups. In River Front City, Wisconsin, the home town of one of the authors, the Polish Catholic majority is still regarded by the Anglo-Saxon North European Protestants as displaying ethnicity whereas the latter group does not. Anyone who has tried to convince high school students that roast beef is an 'ethnic' food will understand what we mean. The same students are quite willing to recognize that spaghetti and any other form of pasta is an ethnic food that has been taken over by the mainstream but roast beef and other foods of clearly Anglo-Saxon and North European origin are not so regarded. Ethnicity seems to be something ascribed to other people

Figure 2.1 American ethnicity

ETHNICITY	Native American	Asian	Hispanic	African	European non-ethnic	European ethnic
NATIONALITY		Chinese Japanese Korean Laotian Vietnamese Other	Mexican Cuban Central American South American Puerto Rican	Various West Indian North American Black	Mixed European English Scottish/Irish German Scandinavian	Italian Irish Polish French German Eastern European – Jewish Western European – Jewish
RELIGION	Catholic Protestant Mormon Traditional native Other	Buddhist Protestant Other	Catholic	Catholic Protestant Muslim	Protestant MAINSTREAM AMERICA	Catholic Eastern Orthodox Fundamentalist Sects

Figure 2.2 Ethnic Make-Up of US Population

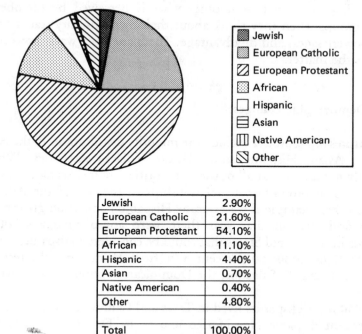

Jewish	2.90%
European Catholic	21.60%
European Protestant	54.10%
African	11.10%
Hispanic	4.40%
Asian	0.70%
Native American	0.40%
Other	4.80%
Total	100.00%

Source: US Bureau of Census Service, 1970

depending upon one's vantage point, excepting when ethnicity is used as a source of identity that serves personal, social or political purposes.

We now move to a relatively simple chart (Figure 2.2) which expresses the major subdivisions of American society by ethnicity. Figure 2.2 expresses in proportions the distribution of characteristics presented in the Figure 2.1.

The largest segment — North European or Anglo-Saxon Protestant — shown in the 1970 Census Report, was approximately 54 per cent of the total US population. This is the category that is most often thought of as 'mainstream' but this is not an adequate reference. The mainstream can be thought of as larger, in the sense that many people who are not North-European or Anglo-Saxon Protestant exhibit behaviors, aspirations, beliefs, and values, that place them in the mainstream culture.

The concept of 'mainstream' may also be enlarged by including European Catholics. When Protestants and Catholics are combined they together make a clear majority of around three-quarters of the total American population. 'Mainstream' is often thought of in this way — as being those persons of predominantly Caucasian ancestry irrespective of religious identification. By adding, for this reason, the Jewish population of about 2.5 per cent, the concept of a majority, mainstream, dominant

American population becomes even more manifest. It seems that this overwhelming majority is sometimes what is perceived by members of minority groups when they think about their own minority status and its relative powerlessness and disadvantage. There are other ways, however, of looking at the matter.

Demographic changes

Other features of Figure 2.2 include the minority distributions in the Native American, Asian, Hispanic, and 'African' (Black) categories. What is particularly notable is that all of these minorities are increasing in absolute numbers and in proportionate relationships to the rest of the American population. For example if we examine Hispanic population growth since 1950 we find that in that year there were approximately 4,000,000 individuals in the United States that could be considered Hispanic. By 1985 there were 17,600,000: 60 per cent were from Mexico and the rest from Puerto Rico, Cuba, El Salvador, the Dominican Republic, Colombia, and Venezuela.

In 1950 most Hispanics lived in Texas and California. In 1985 Arizona was 16 per cent Hispanic, New Mexico 36 per cent, Denver, Colorado 19 per cent, Hartford, Connecticut 20 per cent, Miami 78 per cent.

This is a predominantly young population with a median age of twenty-three and a very high fetility rate. There is an increasing flow of Hispanic immigrants as well. By the year 2000 it is estimated that there will be somewhere between 30,000,000 and 35,000,000 Hispanics in the United States constituting about 12 per cent of the total population. It will be the largest non-Black minority and will clearly outnumber people of many other ethnic backgrounds.

Other minority populations are growing almost as rapidly. The Asian population, though exhibiting a lower birth rate, has been swelled by immigration. The numbers on the chart must already be corrected to about 5.0 per cent of the total population (1986) of 236,182,860. The Native American population likewise is growing, though it will remain a relatively small minority of the total. After the coming of Europeans to North America the Native American population suffered drastic declines due to both disease and military action, though the former was much more devastating. This population has risen from around 300,000 at the turn of the century to about 1,500,000 at present. The proportion of Native Americans in the total American population probably amounts to about 0.6 per cent. It is very difficult, however, to obtain accurate information on the actual number of Native Americans in the US since many individuals who are of mixed Native

American ancestry no longer identify themselves as Native American. On the other hand, many individuals who have only a small amount of Native American inheritance do claim this ethnic designation. This tendency is noted in all minority populations in America. Consequently, all figures and proportions must be regarded as approximate.

The Black population is also increasing rapidly due to a high birth rate but not by significant immigration, excepting for Haitians. For that reason the Hispanic and Asian populations will increase proportionately in relationship to the whole more rapidly than the Black population. The Black population at present (1980 Census) constitutes about 12 per cent of the total. These proportions are presented in Figure 2.3.

The combination of a high birth rate and, in some categories, also high immigration, is resulting in an overall proportionate increase in the minority categories just discussed. It is probable that by the year 2000 the so-called 'minorities' will constitute about one-third of the total US population. It is possible that in the last half of the twenty-first century, the 'minorities' will be the majority. In many schools in urban areas the students of 'minority' status already constitute the majority.

Demographic projections for California, now the most populous state in the union, show dramatic changes in the proportions of non-White minorities in relation to Whites. By 1990 the dominance of the White

Figure 2.3 United States Resident Population, by Race/Ethnicity — 1980

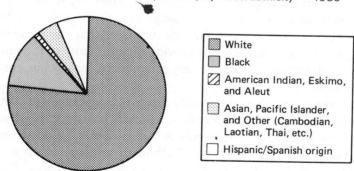

Racial/Ethnic Group:	1980
White	76.60%
Black	11.70%
American Indian, Eskimo, and Aleut (Native American)	0.60%
Asian, Pacific Islander, and Other (Cambodian, Laotian, Thai, etc.)	4.60%
Hispanic/Spanish origin	6.50%

Source: US Bureau of the Census (1981, 1987)

majority will be threatened and by 2020, if present trends continue, a conservative estimate is that the 'minorities' will be the majority. It is not necessarily true that 'as goes California so goes the nation', but the tendencies in this direction have already appeared in many states. Some projections place Whites at less than 50 per cent, Blacks at around 15 per cent, Hispanics at about 22 per cent and Asians around 12 per cent by the year 2080 for the United States as a whole.

However, sheer numbers and even proportions do not tell the whole story. The most important consideration, in the framework we have been developing in this book, is to what extent minorities will have acquired 'mainstream' cultural values, attitudes, and behaviors and attained the concomitant socioeconomic rewards — to what extent they have become full participants in the American cultural dialogue.

Demographic projections are always very tricky and there may be surprises in store for us. The European Protestant, clearly, as well as the Jewish population, and to a lesser extent the European Catholic populations, have all experienced decreasing birth rates in the past several decades. At present, the upper-middle socioeconomic status Protestants are not replacing themselves. This trend towards lower birth rates is notable also for all central and north European countries. A lowering birth rate appears to be associated with increasing educational and economic status. If this is the case we would expect that the 'minority' population we have been discussing will also experience a decreasing birth rate as their educational and socioeconomic status improves. The question, however, is whether or not this improvement will occur rapidly enough to have a significant effect over the next two or three decades. Though it is clear that the socioeconomic status and educational status are improving for a minority of the 'minority' populations, the effect may not be very pronounced for any but a relatively selected group.

In any event, ethnic and minority diversity is a permanent part of the American scene. The question remains, however, how deep this divergence goes and how permanent the depth is. America was founded upon the 'melting pot' ideal. Many persons of ethnic or minority status reject this concept and make attempts to maintain a strong ethnic identity. But at the same time the mass media, the educational system, the culture of the work place, the search for instrumental avenues to power and achievement — the increasing participation in the cultural dialogue — all seem to work against the maintenance of strong separatist or divergent identities.

There are some interesting trends in self-reporting of ethnicity in the 1980 census. There is a growing 'unhyphenated White' population that reports as 'American' rather than of English, German, Irish, Polish, Scandinavian, etc. origin, despite the fact that census takers discourage this

Figure 2.4a Population of California, by Race/Ethnicity — 1970

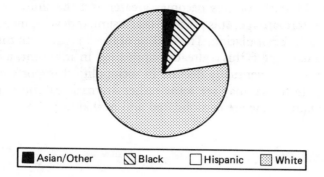

Figure 2.4b Population of California, by Race/Ethnicity — 1990

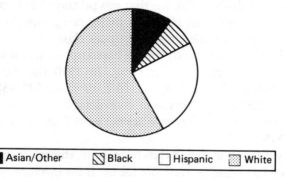

Figure 2.4c Population of California, by Race/Ethnicity — 2020

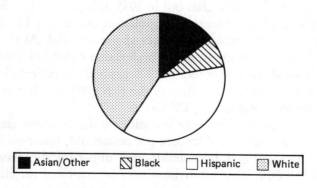

Source: California Department of Finance, 1988

response. This broader and 'non-ethnic' identification occurs as distance in time from old world origins becomes greater and the lines have become blurred by intermarriage. It is possible that a similar development will occur in the non-White population. The decline of race in American thinking and social relations suggests this is already happening. In any event, it is probable that ethnicity will eventually decline in sociopolitical importance, though the immediate future may see some rather dramatic exhibitions of ethnic identity as gains made are consolidated and new aims projected.

Social Class

There is a further and most important subdivision and categorization of the American population, this time by social class as well as by presumed ethnicity. Each of the populations that was portrayed in Figures 2.2 and 2.3 is subdivided by social class into four major categories: lower class, lower-middle class, upper-middle class, and upper class.

These divisions into social class are based upon income and income, like everything else in America, is moving. In 1950 the median income in America per household was $14,832. In 1970 it was $27,338 and in 1985 it was $27,335. Taking inflation into consideration, which is only partially built into the figures just given, we are not as well off in our country today as we were in 1950.

It is very difficult to define class by income, though this is about the only figure that we have readily available for us. If for instance we take the range from $15,000 to $49,999 as a contemporary statement of broad middle class economic status, in 1970 about 65 per cent of the American population could be considered middle class but in 1985 only 58 per cent. However, in 1970 13 per cent of the American population made over $50,000 annual income per household, but in 1985 over 18 per cent did. At the same time those households struggling to get by on less that $15,000 increased during this period from about 22 per cent in 1970 to about 24 per cent in 1985. It is clear that there are tendencies toward the rich getting richer and the poor getting poorer in contemporary US society.

In terms of present levels of incomes we define lower class as being below $15,000 a year annual income per household; lower-middle class as $15,000 to $30,000 per household; and upper-middle class as above $30,000 to $50,000. This subdivision may be criticized for eliminating a middle-middle class. The logic for this is that persons of over $30,000 per year income per household are aspiring to upper-middle class status even though they may not have achieved it. This swells the ranks of the upper-middle class and we could well designate an upper-upper middle class with incomes of over $50,000 per household to $150,000.

This still leaves us with the problem of the upper class. There are several ways of defining this group. One of the easiest ways would be to simply say that upper class incomes are inherited. What is wrong with this is the fact that there are hundreds of new millionaires in America each year; do we have to wait for the children to inherit their parents' wealth to include them in the upper class? Would we include those individuals who are acknowledged by others in their community as upper class? In short 'upper class' is a status which is difficult to define in American society. We will simply define it as those individuals with more than $150,000 annual household income. This actually includes a number of individuals who in terms of attitudes and values, work habits, and so forth are clearly upper-middle class and some who are even lower class. They have simply succeeded in producing more income than most other members of a broadly conceived middle class.

The most important single observation is that all groups or categories defined as Jewish, European Catholic, European Protestant, Black, Hispanic, Asian, Native American, are distributed throughout all social classes defined on socioeconomic terms existing in the contemporary US. There are upper-middle class persons in every category, and there are lower-middle class and lower class persons. That there are upper class persons is problematic for the reasons that we have stated.

In any event this distribution suggests that there is greater mobility in American society than some analysts would have it. Though there is unfairness in the distribution, there is apparently the chance for a high income and status achievement irrespective of ethnicity.

Notes

The census data for figure 2.2 are derived from the US Bureau of Census Service (1970), and for figure 2.3 from the US Bureau of Census (1981, 1987). The data for Hispanics are from McCarthy and Valdez (1985, 1986 see bibliography for Chapter 9, by H. Trueba), the U.S. Department of Commerce (1987), the California Department of Finance (1983), and US Department of Commerce (1980).

The data for figures 2.4a, 2.4b, and 2.4c are abstracted from the California Department of Finance (1988). Trends in self-reporting ethnicity are from Lieberman and Waters (1988). Social class projections and income are derived from the United States Department of Commerce (1988) and from Parker (1972). Fussell (1983) provides an amusing, non-scientific but often painfully accurate view of the 'American Status System'. DeVos (1980) provides an illuminating discussion of ethnicity and minority status.

Chapter 3

American Mainstream Culture

Introduction

There are some ambiguities about mainstream culture that we are not going to be able to resolve effectively, but we can take some steps towards a better understanding of that culture and the difficulties in defining its loci. We still have not precisely defined who is included in mainstream. If we take a conventional view of the matter, we can define mainstream as simply European (including Anglo-Saxon) Protestant. This would include a little over half of the total American population. However, many persons of European Catholic ancestry would have every reason to resent being left out. If we include them we have a total of around 75 per cent of the population of the United States. But certainly persons who identify themselves as Jews could object to being left out of the mainstream since their habits and values seem to be those that we think of as characteristically American. If we add them we get a slight increase in the three-quarters majority. However other significant segments of the other so-called minorities, the Blacks, Hispanics, Asians and Native Americans must be included using these criteria. To the extent that individuals in these categories display behaviors and hold values or beliefs or maintain attitudes that we think of as being characteristically American they are certainly no less American than anyone from any of the other categories.

Taken from this point of view, the mainstream includes anyone who acts like a member of the mainstream, dominant American population and has the income to support this lifestyle. In some respects, this is the most workable and least invidious definition of mainstream and perhaps we should leave the matter there.

There are, however, some advantages in doing a further dissection of the mainstream population. We have no interest in trying to demonstrate the alleged superiority or inferiority of anyone, but we believe that there is a useful model that can be generated by further analysis. This model will be of relationships within the functioning totality of the American society.

Mainstream Cultural Values

A first useful step in this further analysis will be to identify the characteristic value orientations that we think of as mainstream. In our pretest, described in the previous chapter, respondents are asked to define the 'core' American values that they themselves hold. There are five major value orientations listed. They are: freedom of speech (and other forms of personal freedom); the rights of the individual (to be an individual and act in his or her own behalf); equality (as equality of opportunity and including sexual equality); the desirability of achievement attained by hard work (and the belief that anyone can achieve success if he or she works hard enough); and social mobility (the assumption that anyone can improve social status because the social structure is open and hard work will get you there). 'Democracy', as a word, is rarely used but upon discussion it turns out that respondents think of those characteristic features listed as constituting democracy.

There are also a number of other specific values that are listed by a significant number of respondents. They include: a belief in the efficacy of American technology and its ability to solve even the problems it creates; the desirability of a free market with no restraints placed upon it for any reasons except possibly those connected with environmental destruction; the value placed upon private business, closely related to the strong belief in the rights of the individual. Independence is frequently mentioned but seems to be subsumed by the value placed upon the individual and his or her rights. The individual has a right to be independent of constraints placed by higher authority but also to be independent economically. Respect for others is frequently listed, usually in a context of either individuality or equality. Surprisingly, competition is infrequently mentioned. When competition is mentioned it is within the context of individuality, freedom and equality.

It is interesting that there is no significant association between expression of the value orientations that we have listed and one's definition of one's self as a member of a minority or an ethnic group. There are some tendencies for male and female respondents to profile a little differently on respect for others, which females mention more frequently, and equality, particularly sexual equality, which females also mention more frequently.

It is a big leap, too big for sound social science, to ascribe value orientations expressed by a few hundred college-age respondents to the American population as a whole. We regard these tendencies as expressed here as only suggestive. We do, however have a much larger sample collected with a different technique that we will call a 'values projective technique'. We will discuss the results of the application of this technique to a much larger sample in this chapter as well.

The data that we have described point toward a values profile that is not too unexpected but is what we would expect on the basis of common knowledge of the American scene. It may constitute a unifying orientation for a population actually composed of quite divergent elements as it is entirely possible for people to agree upon certain prominent orientations of this kind which are ideological as well as cultural or personal, and at the same time diverge considerably from each other in many other areas of belief, attitude and habit. True to our notion of cultural dialogue, the agreement on these apparently core value orientations would be at the center of the dialogue. In a conversation, an editorial, a public policy, a discussion of American history, and so forth, we would make the assumption that all who engage in the dialogue would ascribe, in general terms at least, to these value orientations. When an individual, out of political commitment or personal cynicism expresses a contrary position we tend to get agitated and defensive. If you do not think this is so, declare yourself in the next discussion that provides a relevant context as being against freedom of speech, rights of the individual, equality, particularly sexual equality, a work ethic and the possibility of attaining success.

This exercise has not helped us define the numerical proportions of the mainstream, but it has helped to define some cultural characteristics that we can think of as subsumed by this concept. We need, however, to take the analysis further.

Profiles and Trends in American Dialogue about Cultural Values

Towards the end of this chapter we will attempt to define more precisely some alternative definitions of 'mainstream' value orientations that seem significant in the American cultural dialogue. We will base our discussion in the following pages on a mass of data that we began to collect from Stanford University students in 1952 and have continued to collect each year through 1990; These data have been collected from all classes of undergraduates as well as all years of graduate students. We have also collected the same kind of data from students at the University of Wisconsin at Madison, University of California at Santa Barbara, the University of Alaska at Fairbanks, San Francisco University, and Sonoma State University. Interestingly enough, the data from these separate sources profile in much the same way. Of course we are drawing from a relatively narrow age range even though graduate students are included, but we are not selecting from as narrow a socioconomic status range as might be suggested by the college or university status of the respondents. Nor are we eliminating minority group representatives because of the college or university sites. The sex ratio is slightly in favor of females since more of our respondents are in social science and education courses, but all departments and schools are represented.

We also have samples from other parts of the country collected by other persons and from quite different regional and social economic distributions. Bernice McAllister has collected responses from individuals on the West Coast including high school and elementary school students, teachers, parents, and school board members. Samples of junior high school respondents and East Coast respondents not in school have been collected. Richard Navarro has collected a sample from students at Michigan State University. We cannot claim that any of these samples or the sample population in its totality are without socioeconomic, ideological, or cultural bias. However, the fact that there are no consistent differences between the distributions of these responses from these different samples lends credence to the notion that the samples do reflect a consistent and pervasive American dialogue.

It is also relevant that in previous researches by the American College Examination Board including 200,000 freshmen in 350 colleges, universities and junior colleges there is substantial evidence to indicate that the kinds of values and their distribution produced by the application of our values projection technique are indeed very widespread. It is particularly important for our purposes that minority students do not differentiate from 'Anglo' students in their responses. In fact, minority students tend to be more oriented to the presumed core values than are mainstream students.

The values projective technique is supplied at the end of this chapter. It consists of twenty-four open-ended sentences and a request for a paragraph describing the ideal American. You can administer it to yourself, to a friend, or to your students, if you are a teacher, or you could even use it for a parlor game. It is not a personality test so it is not as dangerous to play with as a Rorschach inkblot test or a Minnesota Multiphasic Personality Inventory might be.

The questions were initially produced in 1952 on the basis of writings by anthropologists about American culture. These sources are listed at the end of this book under References. These analyses exhibit a high degree of commonality; coming from quite different disciplinary persuasions and backgrounds of personal experience these anthropologists, concerned with American character and culture, seem to have arrived at about the same interpretations.

From their interpretations, we formulated a number of open-ended sentences. When we administer the technique we ask respondents to complete the sentence with the first thing that comes to mind. Since the first thing that comes to mind is not always the statement that an individual would wish to stand by, we also given respondents an opportunity to argue with themselves after the technique has been completed. Surprisingly few respondents actually do so.

Most of the incomplete sentences in the technique center directly upon attributes defined in the listed anthropological interpretations such as 'all men are born _____.', 'honesty is _____', 'the individual is _____', 'in order to be successful one has to _____', 'time is _____'. There are a number of other responses that are less directly related to these attributes such as 'artists are _____, 'intellectuals should _____', 'college professors should _____' and 'nudity is _____'. Responses to every one of the twenty-four incomplete sentences appear to be culturally patterned and seem to have a lot to do with a core configuration of values that we can describe as mainstream and American.

Constant Features

There are certain value orientations that have appeared consistently over the entire period of the administration of the technique. These constant features taken together would seem to constitute a core cultural configuration that constitutes the center of the American dialogue. Those features exhibiting the most continuity through time are: equality; honesty (as the best policy); the value of work coupled with clear goals; the significance of the self-reliant individual; and sociability — getting along well with others and being sensitive to their needs and appraisals. The incomplete sentences on the values projective techniques that have produced the most consistent results are (2) All men are born —, (4) Honesty is —, (5) Anyone can get to the top if they —, (9) The most successful people —, (14) What counts is what a person —, (15) It isn't a person's background that counts it's what —, (16) The individual is —, (18) In order to be successful one has to —, It isn't what one says that counts it is what one —, (22) Time is —, (23) There's no use crying —. Taking these sentences alone as a statement of the American core value configuration we can state the following: All men are born equal. Honesty is the best policy. Anyone can get to the top if they work hard enough. The most successful people worked hard to become so. It isn't a person's background that counts it is what he or she is or does. The individual is all-important, unique, and supreme. In order to be successful one has to work hard and keep trying. It isn't what one says that counts, it is what one really does. Time is of the essence and very precious. And there is no use crying over spilled milk (this is often recorded in the more archaic form 'spilt' milk). If phrased in a more literary form this could be regarded as a statement of the American credo.

It is important to remember that we are thinking of these value orientations as being a part, not the totality, of the American dialogue. When we say that they are a part of the American dialogue, we mean that we talk about them, sometimes explicitly as in arguing for public works or political positions or implicitly as we enter in discussions assuming that values of this kind are held by the others with whom we are in conversation.

In the political campaigns for the presidency in 1952, Edward Steele examined in great detail all of the campaign speeches by Dwight D. Eisenhower and Adlai Stevenson. These two men were presumably quite opposed to each other. Stevenson represented the liberal (from some points of view, quite radical left) and Eisenhower the conservative (from some points of view, quite radical right) positions then current on the American ideological and political scene. The value orientations explicitly expressed by both Stevenson and Eisenhower were virtually identical. Both of the candidates used the very points that we have presented as the basis for value oriented statements in their campaign speeches. They even made them at about the same times so that one would, presumably, not be left behind the other. As far as the American public is concerned it had no choice between value orientations. Whatever differences the two candidates were able to express were expressed with these value orientations as a consensus. This is precisely what we mean by an American cultural dialogue. Whether there is conflict or agreement, these value orientations are pivots around which the dialogue occurs.

The dialogue consists of the pivotal value orientations *and* the oppositions to them. Every one of the incomplete sentences also evokes negative or oppositional responses. The opposition to 'The individual is all-important', for example, includes 'The individual is nothing by himself (or herself)'; 'The individual is important only as a member of a group (or society, community)'. 'In order to be successful one has to work hard (or unceasingly, energetically, etc.)', is opposed with 'know the right people', 'step on others', 'look out for number one'.

Oppositions are not only between persons of differing orientations but within individuals. They may operate at an intellectual level but often appear to constitute emotionally laden issues and affect personal adjustment. Oppositions also appear to be reflected in cycles of change over time in our sample, and they are reflected in longer range changes in the history of our country.

The nature of culture, as the anthropological structuralists maintain, is that meanings are possible because there are oppositions. Clean is only understandable in contrast to dirty, dark to white, good to bad, positive to negative. If God is dead in some quarters it is because we have done away with the devil. If oppositions are that essential to meaning, and the actions we take in the framework of meaning, it is inevitable that the pivotal value orientations we are analyzing contain and evoke oppositions. The meaning of the positive response to any one of the incomplete sentences must be understood in order to produce a negative response, an opposition.

Changes in Value Orientations

There are some value orientations that were strong in 1952 that have undergone considerable change over the more than three decades that data have been collected using this technique.

For example, in 1952 through about 1964 the major response to incomplete sentence twelve, 'the future is', was 'exciting', 'challenging', 'hopeful', 'a time of opportunity'. The sentence completions were overwhelmingly optimistic and optimism about the future was considered by the anthropological writers on American culture of that time and previously as being a salient and consistent American cultural characteristic.

Today there are two kinds of response to this incomplete sentence that were not there in significant numbers in 1952 to 1964. They are: (1) 'the future is before us', or 'The future is unknown'. These responses are non-committal. They acknowledge that the future is coming but they refrain from either a positive and optimistic or negative appraisal of its characteristics. (2) A negative, pessimistic response: 'The future is threatening'; 'The future is uncertain'; 'The future is ending'. Frequently, as respondents elaborate their response they define the future as uncertain because of the possibilities of nuclear war or the terminal pollution of our living environment. The optimism of the earlier period has eroded. The optimistic view of the future is, however, still a significant category. About 40 per cent of all who respond fall in this category. In the 1950s and early 1960s it was closer to 80 per cent.

It is important to realize that the dialogue itself is still about the future in this particular instance, but the content of the dialogue has changed to suit the circumstances of life in America and on our globe during the most recent decades. There has been a slight increase in the number of optimistic responses since 1987 but it is too short a time and too small a sample to make assertive statements about another possible change.

Another important change has occurred with respect to attitudes about and values concerning nonconformity. In the earlier period (1952–1964) the third sentence, 'artists are', was completed by a minority of about 25 per cent as 'artists are queer', 'artists are jerks', 'artists are eccentric', 'artists are nuts', 'artists are effeminate'. This category of response has virtually disappeared from samples since 1966. Artists are now considered to be 'unique', 'creative', 'productive', 'individuals'. Artists may be considered within the traditional framework of American values as deviant because they are not primarily engaged with material and economic production. Being an artist seemed to many people to be a kind of 'copout' from the necessary and major work of our society. This attitude, which was held by a significant minority of respondents in the college age population that we sampled, seems to have virtually disappeared. This is only one index, to be sure, of a much more complex development, but it is suggestive. Perhaps attitudes towards nonconforming behaviors and individuals have become more tolerant and open during the most recent decades.

The same comments can be made about the open ended sentence 'Intellectuals should'. In the earlier period about 30 per cent of the respondents saw intellectuals in very undesirable terms: 'Intellectuals should drop dead'; 'Intellectuals should keep it under cover'; 'Intellectuals should keep their mouths shut'. There is a high degree of consistency between the statement about artists and about intellectuals. Both may be regarded as deviant within the American cultural scene and perhaps for the same reasons. Both artists and intellectuals have stepped out of the mainstream orientation towards economic and material production. An intellectual point of view is often considered introspective, withdrawn, or noninvolved.

There is also the suspicion that intellectuals can cause trouble because they challenge existing assumptions and turn the heads of their students, if they happen to be teachers, in potentially dangerous directions. One can find examples of this orientation in the mass media such as tabloids which from time to time publish 'news' items about the pernicious influences of liberal college professors upon American youth.

Perhaps most important as a contribution to the negative appraisal of intellectuals is the notion that intellectuals set themselves not only apart but regard themselves as superior to others. Americans tend to be suspicious of anyone who does not profess equality, meaning (in America) sameness and nonexceptionability. Political candidates try hard to convince us all that they are just regular fellows by using poor language, donning work uniforms (or at least hard hats) and shaking hands with, and hugging almost anybody that seems to be willing to offer their hands or bodies for such contact. If one is an expert about anything in America, it is best to express humility and emphasize basic human commonness. The reduction of this negative category in the college age population would seem to suggest some loosening up of previous orientations and reactions to some forms of nonconformity.

Closely related to the changes that we have noted there is another that offhand does not seem particularly important. 'Nudity is —' in the earlier period was responded to by a sizable minority as 'obscene', 'vulgar', or, in one form or another as 'immoral'. There are currently two major responses to this question. One is that nudity is 'beautiful', 'free', 'exciting', 'fun' and so on — all positive and a majority female response. The other major response type is context-oriented: 'Nudity is o.k. with the right people'; 'Nudity is sometimes embarrassing'; 'Nudity is all right in its place'. There is, in fact, another response category of some significance and that is a humorous one: 'Nudity is cold in a winter climate'; 'Nudity is a good way to get bitten by insects'.

The point here is that again there seems to have been the development of a more tolerant attitude, this time not towards nonconformity so much as towards a moral position. Certainly canons of respectability have shifted considerably of late. Bathing costumes for young females seem to have gone as far as they can without divesting one's self of them entirely. Nude scenes are included in movies and now even appear occasionally on television. There are legitimate nude beaches around most coastal urban centers. We seem to have been developing more tolerance and a more relativistic cultural attitude towards behaviors that would have been considered to be nonconforming and even immoral at an earlier time by a significant minority of respondents.

Another very important area of change has been in respect to the connection between work, success and achievement. In the earlier period, anyone could get to the top if he or she tried, or worked hard enough, and the most successful people worked hard to become so, and certainly one had to work hard in order to become successful. Although such responses still dominate there is an increasing cynicism about this connection. During some years as many as 50 per cent of the respondents express deep cynicism about this relationship: 'Anyone can get to the top if he or she cheats or steps on people'; 'The most successful people arrive there on the backs of others'. This 'cynical' opposition has always been in the dialogue but is expressed more frequently of late.

There is another trend connected with this pivotal area that is not primarily cynical. There seems to have been a shift from a concern with work and success in its external form to the development of inner resources and peace and even happiness within one's self: 'In order to be successful one has to be at peace with one's self'; 'The most successful people know themselves'.

There was a time during the late 1960s and early 1970s when even the feted American individualism was being challenged. Although the dominant response from the beginning of the administration of the technique to the present has been that the individual has been important, or even 'sacred' or 'supreme', there has always been a minority that regard the individual essentially as a member of the community: 'The individual is important only as a member of the community or of the group'. This response category waned during the 1980s.

In fact the most recent change in the distribution of responses to the values projective technique as a whole has been in what can be described as a conservative direction. Work, success, achievement, and individualism are stated in ways very similar to the 1952 sample. During the period 1965 to approximately 1974 there was a strong movement towards less emphasis upon success and its linkage with hard work, less emphasis on the individual, and more interest in self development, more concern for other people and their needs, a more relativistic conception of order and morality, less certainty that the time-honored formula of work to get ahead will be successful and more suspicion of authority, than there is at the present time.

However this cycling back to a more conservative cultural position does not place the present generation of respondents in the framework of the same values profile as in 1952 to 1964. Though there has been a lessening of the trends just noted and a relative emphasis on the earlier formulas, it is true that the present generation of respondents is more tolerant of nonconformity, more interested in self development, more concerned for other people and their needs, more relativistic, than the 1952 to 1964 respondents were.

The inclusion of tolerance and relativism, self development, concern for others, is particularly clear in the paragraphs about the 'ideal American'. This ideal person should have 'clear goals', 'determination', be willing to 'work hard' in the attainment of goals, be 'intelligent', and 'competent', but also exhibit 'concern for others', including those less fortunate. He or she should be 'sensitive' to others' needs, and exhibit a 'caring' nature. He or she should also have an inner 'peace and happiness', 'know oneself', and know 'who they are'.

It appears that these kind of value orientations, dominant in the 1960s and 1970s, have been retained but coupled with a return to the work and success ethic. These values have always been present in the American dialogue and are accentuated or recede with the times. Philanthropy, altruism, and concern for others less fortunate than oneself have been American habits of the mind since pre-Revolutionary times.

These 'cycles' seem to be the nature of cultural change in a dynamic society like ours. We can expect cyclic changes and some of the cycle will take us back to a previous position, but in the transition from one position to another the attributes picked up on the way through time become a part of the whole dialogue. It is, then, a matter of relative emphasis upon certain value orientations, certain aspects of the dialogue at different times. Presumably these different emphases are responses to the real conditions of life during these times. Value orientations and the dialogue about them are never fixed. They must be considered to be adaptations that make it possible for people to make sense out of their environment, and each other, and maintain motivation. In short, those features exhibiting the most continuity through time are: equality; honesty as the best policy; the value of work coupled with clear goals; the significance of the self-reliant individual; and getting along well with others and being sensitive to their needs and appraisals. Those features exhibiting the greatest shift in meaning and value are: optimism about the future; tolerance of nonconformity; and the value of material success.

The changes in response modalities over time exhibit a trend that can be described as progressively less traditional, if we take the statement of cultural ideology furnished above as our starting point. The changes have been in the following directions: more tolerance for nonconformity, more interest in self development than rugged individualism, more concern for people and their needs, a more relativistic conception of order and morality, less certainty that the philosophy 'work to get ahead' will indeed work at all, and more suspicion of authority.

In the late 1970s and 1980s there has been a swing back towards the traditional formula. Work, success, achievement and individualism as stated in the samples between 1979 and the present do exhibit similarities to the 1952–1964 samples. However it does appear that certain attributes such as a more relativistic attitude, more tolerance toward nonconformity and more interest in inner and self development have been incorporated in the profile. Though less emphasized at present than in the period between 1965 and 1974, they appear to be a constant part of the dialogue.

Our discussion has helped us to understand a little better the qualitative features of the mainstream American dialogue and the pivotal value areas that it centers around, but it has not permitted us to be more specific about the size or composition of mainstream populations. We will try to consider this in the next section as we attempt to define mainstream further and call attention to a concept that we will call 'referent ethni-class'. This is going to be difficult for one of the features of the American system is that there are relatively few acknowledged boundaries between groups of people based upon culturally patterned behaviors.

The Referent Ethniclass

Figure 3.1 locates mainstream America in the European Protestant, 'non-ethnic' categories and further specifies the mainstream to be composed of the lower-middle and upper-middle socioeconomic classes. This is a narrow definition of mainstream. As we have pointed out, the cultural distribution of mainstream characteristics extends far beyond the Protestant, North European, Anglo-Saxon middle class. In the broadest sense of the term, mainstream America is constituted of all persons irrespective of ethnicity or religion or social class who exhibit mainstream cultural characteristics. However, for the purposes of our analysis at the moment we will define mainstream as the chart defines it.

Figure 3.1 American Ethnicity and the Mainstream

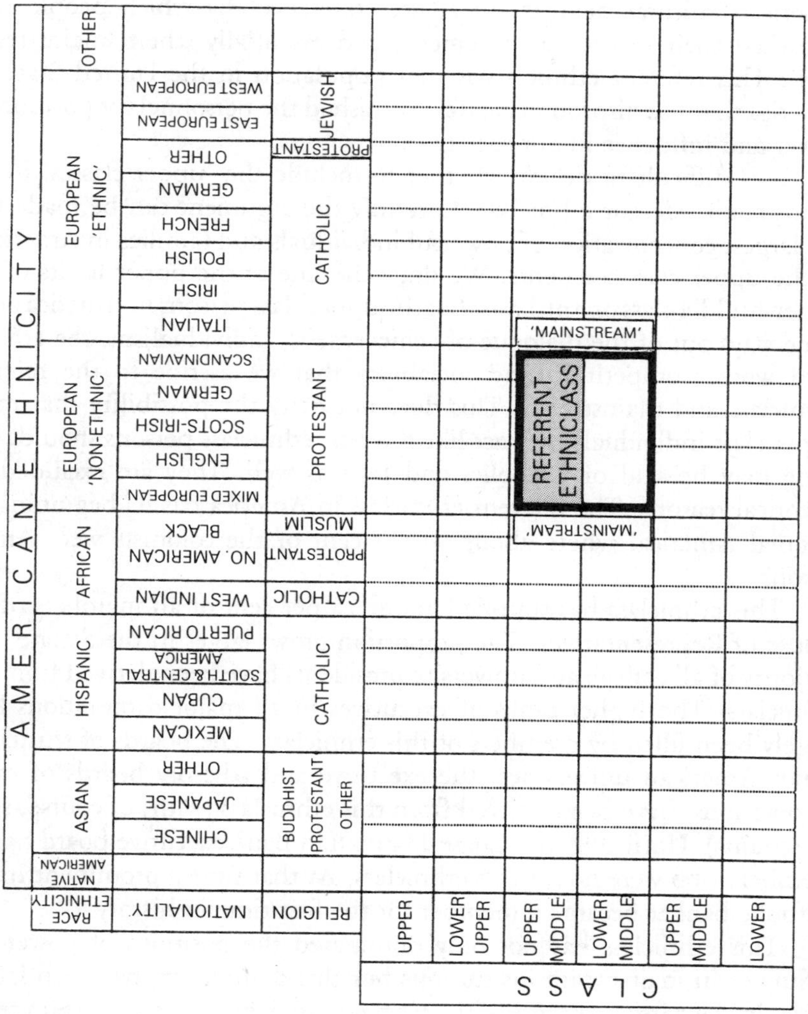

*From The Ethnicity of White 'Non-Ethics,' by Louise Bay Waters

We need to make a further limitation meaningful and that is the designation of a referent ethniclass. This ethniclass consists of part of the portion marked mainstream on the chart above and that part is the upper-middle social class of the European, 'nonethnic', Protestant category. Our argument here is that this upper-middle segment of the historically defined American cultural mainstream is the 'reference' by which people have measured their success, achievement, and essentially, their 'mainstream-ness'. This referent ethniclass is that population in the United States of America that has disproportionately furnished the personnel for positions of power and influence in our society.

It is difficult to decide whether to include the 'upper classes' in the mainstream referent ethniclass. Certainly the argument can be made that the largest concentration of powerful individuals and families in America is in the upper class segments. We draw the line at the upper limits of the upper-middle class on the basis that the upper class persons in America are in some ways out of the dialogue of achievement, individualism, the ethic of hard work, competition and sociability that we ascribe to the referent ethniclass and mainstream. This does not deny the possibility that many upper class individuals may act like referent ethniclass persons should. The same may be said of Catholics and Jews as well. They are excluded for historical reasons. The referent ethniclass in America has its beginnings in colonial America, where about 60 per cent of the colonists were Anglo-Saxons.

This ethniclass has supplied about 75 per cent of all members of the House of Representatives. The proportion grows larger in the Senate. The majority of all college and university presidents have been derived from this ethniclass. The higher ranks of executives in all major corporations have largely been filled by members of this ethniclass. The boards of trustees of major American universities, the executive and advisory boards of major corporations, have been derived from this ethniclass (with, of course, some exceptions). Until 1985 the Chase-Manhattan Bank executive board had no members who were not of this ethniclass. At that time a prominent Italian Catholic banker became a member for the first time in history.

This ethniclass has not only dominated the positions of power and influence in mainstream institutions but this domination has been largely male. In the narrowest sense of the term we can define the mainstream center as referent and male dominated — an ethniclass constituted of a minority of European, 'nonethnic', Protestants.

In this restricted sense there is a ruling class in America; one could almost say 'caste'. It is historically defined and of long standing. It emerged in pre-Revolutionary times and has maintained its position into the present. There is no question that this power position has eroded somewhat of late.

There are positions of power and influence occupied by members of every social class and every kind of ethnicity. Furthermore, women have made significant movement into such positions. Though this is certainly true, it does not seem that the central positions in the most important contexts have been usurped by a large number of individuals representing other than the referent ethniclass.

Nevertheless, there is movement and change. For the first time in American history a Black, Jesse Jackson, made a significant move in 1988 toward candidacy for the highest office of the US and the ethnicity of the Democratic candidate, Michael Dukakis, was not that of the referent ethniclass either, though his behaviors are. The President of the United States elected in 1988, George Bush, is a very solid representative of the referent ethniclass. It is interesting also, that women seemed to be making significant moves into the politics of power with the candidacy of Geraldine Ferraro for Vice President in 1984. In the election of 1988, however, women were not particularly visible in the higher echelons of politics. One needs only to look at the composition of the personnel 'on stage' to see that this is true. We seem, as usual, to be moving in several directions at once. This may be one of the most important strengths and possibly one of the weaknesses of the American way of doing things.

A Model for American Cultural Relations

Drawing upon the previous discussions of social class, ethnicity, values, and dialogue, we will attempt construction of a central model for cultural relations in America. This model places the referent ethniclass culture at the center of the mainstream and arranges all other groups in America in relationship to it. In the interest of clarity only a few segments of the total population are represented. The diagram of this model (Figure 3.2) is not intended as a statement of precise measurement of any kind. Rather, it presents an idea. It is a statement of presumed relationships between and among groups that constitute significant segments of the American population. The rest of this chapter is an explanation of these relationships.

We have defined the mainstream cultural dialogue in America by reference to pivotal value orientations and the referent ethniclass as a subset of the total mainstream population. For the purposes of our model we defined 'mainstream' as consisting of all North European, Anglo-Saxon, Protestant middle class groups and populations. This is not intended as a denial of the mainstream quality of life for representatives of any other group. It does, however, define a 'center', historically derived, with which

Figure 3.2   A Model of American Cultural Relations: the mainstream minorities interaction and the dialogue

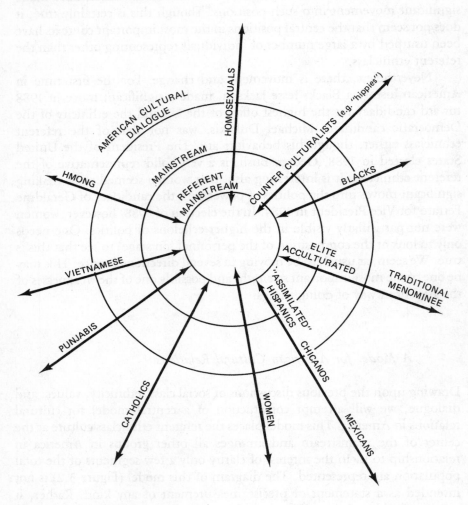

Source: G. and L. Spindler

all groups are in some degree of accord or conflict, including White Catholics and Jews.

The model conveys the idea that all groups in America participate in the American cultural dialogue and that at the the same time a very critical aspect of that dialogue is conflict. The intermediation of this conflict, the accommodation of groups with various origins and various cultural orientations is central to the American cultural dialogue.

Cultural Attributes

The model that we are developing is highly schematic and we have said that it is not intended to be a statement of measured values with any quantitative implications. However, to make our discussion sensible, we need to state the salient cultural features of the mainstream and referent ethniculture. We have tried, in our discussion of value orientations, to paint the picture with broad strokes.

The mainstream cultural value orientations include an emphasis upon the individual and individualism, upon personal achievement and success gained by hard work, equality of opportunity, the value of honesty (as an expedient best policy), a belief in the openness of the American socioeconomic structure that can be penetrated by personal commitment and hard work, a belief in progress, a persistent belief in the future as a time of promise and positive developments (an orientation that has been, as we pointed out, eroded of late), and a sociable, get-along-well-with-others orientation.

In general terms these are the value orientations towards which individuals tend to move during their accommodation to the center of the American cultural dialogue. Whether this means assimilation or not is moot. Though there is considerable rejection of the notion of the 'melting pot' concept, it is undeniable that as ethnic groups become more and more successful at attaining the rewards available through mainstream instrumentalities, they also tend to be culturally assimilated. Mother tongues are lost or decline in use and significance, and clothing styles, personal demeanor, possessions such as homes or other personal property all change in recognizable directions. In a society where as many as 60,000,000 people may be looking at the same television program at the same time, it would be unlikely to be otherwise. There are other influences that are more divisive, such as schools, that we will discuss in Chapter 5.

Nevertheless, individuals may retain significant identities, habits, and ways of thinking that are certainly not mainstream while simultaneously succeeding in adopting mainstream instrumentalities to their own purposes. Our experience with Native American populations has convinced us that various forms of biculturalism are quite workable and, for many persons, may constitute viable adaptations to the need to 'get along' in America at the same time that ethnic pride dictates a retention of self-orientation within one's culture of origin.

The referent ethniclass we define as a variant of the mainstream culture. This class is where success becomes driven, where stratus striving is a dominant fact of life, where the career focus is particularly strong. There are other attributes such as a generalized urban expediency, a disdain for non-affluence and a taste for the mode, (for what is 'trendy') that are apparent in varying degrees and expressed in various ways by subgroups within the referent population. There are of course also regional variations, variations by age and by locale. Uniformity is not, in any American population, an outstanding feature.

In general we can say that the referent ethniclass is an urban professional and business population, college educated, and increasingly characterized in the younger age groups by double incomes. The family style of this young group is characterized by the acronyms, YUPPIES, DINKS and DIOKS (DINKS are double income no kids and DIOKS are double income one kid). This is also a population with a very high divorce rate. The stress engendered by high speed urban business and professional lives within two career families and little to hold the couple together constitutes prime conditions for such a high divorce rate. Among the Stanford 'non-ethnic' respondents to the values projective technique's first statement 'I wish my parents had_____', the sentence completions take two major forms: 'I wish my parents had more money', and 'I wish my parents had stayed together' or 'resolved their differences'.

There are other dimensions of referent culture, shared widely among upper-middle class persons irrespective of ethnicity, that fall under the heading *style*. Speech, humor, courtesies, clothing, possessions of all kinds, home and particularly interior decoration, schools attended (and that children attend, as well as colleges planned), interpersonal contacts, travel and cross-cultural experience, reading, television viewing, and particularly self-presentation, that are acquired as one moves into mainstream class status. They are not the American cultural dialogue. They are expressions of some parts of it, but they are criteria for recognition and acceptance. These stylistic features are difficult to 'pick up' and people aspirant to referent-equivalent mainstream status are often marginalized because they have not fully mastered them. This marginalization is usually subtle, covert, and frustrating. It is not necessarily linked to ethnicity, for Whites, even WASP Whites, encounter the criteria and get marginalized, as they rise economically.

The groups shown in the diagram (3.2) in the field surrounding mainstream and referent culture are in a two way relationship to that culture. They are making moves, as individuals, into mainstream cultural patterns and mainstream socioeconomic status at the same time that elements of mainstream culture are continually moving out towards them through the mass media, through personal contact, and even the packaging of goods that they use. The diffusion of cultural elements, including elements of style, move in the other direction as well. Every ethnic group in America has contributed or is contributing to the composition of mainstream culture.

Black expressions, mannerisms, attitudes, music, images of poverty, feelings of guilt and anxiety, have profoundly affected the American dialogue and to a significant extent, mainstream culture. We have already spoken of the Native American influence. The Asian influence is growing; foods, clothing styles, decoration, even styles of management, are influencing the mainstream and are very much a part of the dialogue. The Hispanic influence is strong, particularly in the West and Southwest, again, in foods and clothing, language, expressions, some aspects of interpersonal relations, and also in architectural styles. It would be a mistake, however, to regard the mainstream and referent ethniclass as a deep cultural mix of elements from each of the major, long-standing ethnic groups in America. From the inside of the designated mainstream, and particularly the referent ethniclass, the elements accepted seem relatively superficial, the base culture seems very 'Anglo', and many people seem interested in keeping it that way. If this were not so there would be little conflict in the dialogue.

The traditional groupings of each of the minority populations retain the greatest degree of separation and distance. In some cases they may do so by an intentional exclusion of mainstream cultural attributes. The same may be said of the minority referent ethniclass, though here what is being excluded are certain (not all) cultural elements and patterns perceived as 'ethnic' or 'lower class'. But no group in America, no matter how exclusive or reclusive, is entirely outside of the American cultural dialogue.

The Hutterites and the Amish are classic examples of an exclusionary adaptation. The Hutterites are a population of some 20,000 persons who came to this country seeking refuge from religious persecution in the nineteenth century. They have retained a communal living orientation and many attributes of the culture that they came to this country with from Europe. They make strenuous efforts to keep what they regard as undesirable aspects of contemporary North American culture out of their communes. The Amish are somewhat similar in that they, like the Hutterites, are Anabaptists (against infant baptism). They do not live in communes but on family farms scattered over the countryside. The Amish also exclude what they think of as undesirable mainstream characteristics. Both the Hutterites and the Amish try hard to remain separate and do so by excluding cultural features from the mainstream.

In a related way the traditional Menominee Indians described in Chapter 6 make an explicit effort to maintain their traditional culture, even in some cases to learn or relearn it so that they can carry it on. They also try to remain separate but are not as strict about rejecting or excluding mainstream cultural features. In contemporary United States society the most traditional elements within minorities retain their character by self-conscious manipulation of symbols and boundaries.

There are always a number of individuals who are somewhere in between the traditional elements of their group and those groups and individuals who have moved further into a mainstream framework. They may be subject to social, economic, and personal problems characteristic of populations who are in the process of accommodation or rejection of any cultural form. And finally, in every minority population, there are a significant number of individuals who have, in effect, become 'mainstreamers'.

There are some 'problem' groups in our diagram such as women, homosexuals, hippies and other counter culturalists, and any other group or population that is nominally a part of the mainstream population and possibly even of the referent subculture but which in some specific way is either disenfranchised or rejected or has purposely set up some cultural distance between themselves and the mainstream referent center. If we carry the analysis far enough we would find ourselves left with a small core of male, adult Protestant middle class persons from who everybody else would be in some degree divergent and in conflict. Though this would be an extreme interpretation of our model it is not illogical.

Whatever the specifics of the relations between the various groups in the field surrounding mainstream culture and the referent subculture, or whatever the specific composition of the groups may be, the complex processes of conflict, accommodation and cultural diffusion that are denoted by the model constitute the key to the American dialogue.

Notes

Changing profiles of value orientations derived from responses to the Spindler Values Projective Technique are reported in Spindler (1955), (1977), and in Spindler and Spindler (1983). Bernice McAllister (1967) and Richard Navarro (personal communication) report responses collected in other areas. Barbara Nay (1974) analyzed value-oriented responses in the Spindler and other samples. The American College Examination Board profiles are reported in Spindler (1977). Writings by anthropologists about American culture that served as a basis for constructing the Values Projective Technique (in 1952) are: Geoffry Gorer (1948), Clyde Kluckhohn (1949), Florence Kluckhohn (1950), Mead (1943), Powdermaker (1950), Bateson, in Ruesch and Bateson (1951), Riesman (1950), Spindler (1948), Warner (1941). Edward Steele (1957) analyzes the value orientations projected by Dwight Eisenhower and Adlai Stevenson in the 1952 U.S. presidential campaign. The terms 'value' and 'value orientation' are used in our discussion despite the archaic quality they are ascribed by some analysts.

Though our emphasis is upon pivotal concerns around which the American dialogue appears to be centered, these concerns subsume value components — attributes about which there is positive or negative affect. The concept 'Referent Ethniclass' as defined by Louise Bay Waters' unpublished paper (1976), is drawn from related materials in Anderson (1970), Parker (1972), Gordon (1964). The comments on referent ethniclass dominance in business and professional life are from Anderson (1970). Class style is semi-facetiously described by Fussell (1983). John Hostetler and Gertrude Huntington describe the Amish (1976) and the Hutterites (1980).

Values Projective Technique

Complete the sentence with the first thing that comes to mind, no matter what it is.

1. I wish my parents had_____.
2. All men are born_____.
3. Artists are_____.
4. Honesty is_____.
5. Anyone can get to the top if they_____.
6. Intellectuals should_____.
7. If I had a son I would want him to_____.
8. College professors should_____.
9. The most successful people_____.
10. Wealthy people should_____.
11. Everyone should want to_____.
12. The future is_____.
13. I wish I had_____.
14. What counts is what a person _____.
15. It isn't a person's background that counts, it is what_____.
16. The individual is_____.
17. Nudity is_____.
18. In order to be successful one has to_____.
19. French night clubs are_____.
20. The standard of living of the laboring classes should_____.
21. It isn't what one says that counts, it is what one_____.
22. Time is_____.
23. There's no use crying_____.
24. Popular people are_____.

Describe in one short paragraph *your* conception of the ideal American.

Copyright — Ethnographics, Box 38, Calistoga, CA 94515
Source: G. and L. Spindler

Chapter 4

Observing America

We have begun to develop some conception of the attributes of the American cultural dialogue and its distribution throughout the various segments of our national population. Our discussions concerning the dialogue have all been based upon contemporary sources of data. This chapter is devoted to the interpretations of observers of America from before the Revolutionary War to the 1950s.

Though we do not think of these observations as having greater truth value than the other sources of information that we have already used, they do have the virtue of both temporal and crosscultural perspective. The observers to be reported are not only a part of our historical interpretation but they are also in many instances foreigners. Foreign views of America have always been titillating to Americans and this taste for foreign criticism and perspective continues right into the present.

What is surprising is the high degree of continuity exhibited in the content of these observations. If we can take them seriously we can say that American culture has exhibited significant continuity for at least 200 years.

M.G. St Jean de Crevecoeur

Jean de Crevecoeur wrote in the early 1770s. He was a Frenchman who began farming in Orange County, New York in 1765 and wrote many letters, published under the title *Letters of an American Farmer*.

Crevecoeur describes the new continent to which he has come and settled:

> ... a modern society offers itself to his (the settler's) contemplation, different from what he had hitherto seen. It is not composed, as in Europe, of great lords who possess everything, and of a herd of people who have nothing. Here are no aristocratical

families, no courts, no kings, no bishops, no ecclesiastical dominion, no invisible power giving to a few a very visible one; no great manufacturers employing thousands, no great refinements of luxury. The rich and the poor are not so far removed from each other as they are in Europe. Some few towns excepted we are all tillers of the earth from Nova Scotia to West Florida. We are a people of cultivators, scattered over an immense territory, communicating with each other by means of good roads and navigable rivers, united by the silken bands of mild government, all respecting the laws, without dreading their power, because they are equitable. We are all animated with a spirit of an industry which is unfettered and unrestrained because each person works for himself. If he travels through our rural districts he views not the hostile castle, and the haughty mansion, contrasted with a clay built hut and miserable cabin, where cattle and men help to keep each other warm and dwell in meanness, smoke, and indigence. A pleasing uniformity of decent competence appears throughout our habitations.

It is clear that Jean de Crevecoeur saw in the new continent, America, an egalitarianism that pleased him mightily. He notes that everyone works for himself in an 'unfettered and unrestrained' manner. And furthermore, he describes a value that has not been mentioned in previous discussion, the value placed upon agrarianism

He goes on in his letters to describe the vastness of the American continent, comments on how long it will take to people it and then comments on the variety and mixture of people already present.

The next wish of the traveler will be to know whence came all these people? They are a mixture of English, Scottish, Irish, French, Dutch, Germans, and Swedes. From this promiscuous breed, that race now called Americans have arisen. The eastern provinces must indeed be accepted, as being the unmixed descendents of Englishmen. I have heard many wish that they had been more intermixed also: for my part I am no wisher, and think it much better as it happened . . . What attachment can a poor European immigrant have for a country where he had nothing? The knowledge of the language, the love of a few kindred as poor as himself were the only cords that tied him: his country is now that which gives him land, bread, protection, and consequence. What then is the American, this new man? He is either a European, or the descendant of a European, hence that strange mixture of blood, which you will find in no other country. I could point out to you a family whose grandfather was an Englishman, whose wife was Dutch, whose son married a French woman, and whose present four sons have now four wives of different nations. Is an American, who, leaving behind him all his ancient prejudices and manners, receives new ones from the new mode of life he has embraced, the new government he obeys, and the new rank he holds? Here individuals of all nations are melted into a new race of men, whose labors and posterity will one day cause great changes in the world.

It is clear that Crevecoeur thought of the new society as a melting pot, an ideal and value that is now clouded by issues and sentiments arising from the conditions of life in the last half of the twentieth century. It is important to realize, however, that the 'melting' was done with peoples who, from an anthropological perspective, were not so very different from each other. To Crevecoeur the English, Scotch, Irish, French, Dutch, Germans, and Swedes seemed to be quite different from each other. Of course they are all representatives of Western European culture. Their languages are essentially dialects when seen in the perspective of world languages. Their cultures are different enough to be interesting to travelers and tourists and they do certainly have separate histories, but in no sense can they be thought of as radically different cultures. The 'melting' was therefore comparatively easy. It is interesting that Crevecoeur makes no mention of the Native Americans, the 'Indians' that had occupied and were still present in the territories occupied by the newcomers. Nor does he mention the Blacks who had been brought even at that early time as slaves into part of the occupied area. It is very possible that Crevecoeur did not really consider them to be fully human. In this sense we have made some positive moves in the past 200 years.

Crevecoeur makes another very interesting point and that is concerning the quick identification as an American and the generation of instant patriotism. The 'poor European immigrant', according to Crevecoeur, is only too glad to leave his mother country behind along with all of the prejudices that were a part of that birth place.

Here the rewards of his industry follow with equal steps the progress of his labor; his labor is founded on the basis of nature, self interest; can one want a stronger allurement? Wives and children who before in vain demanded of him a morsel of bread, now, fat and frolicsome, gladly help their father to clear those fields whence exhuberant crops are to arise to feed and to clothe them all; without any part being claimed, either by a despotic prince, a rich abbot, or a mighty lord. Here religion demands but little of him; a small voluntary salary to the minister, and gratitude to God; can he refuse these? . . . This is an American.

Crevecoeur makes the new land sound like the Garden of Eden both in his descriptions of nature itself and the society that grew up out of the new immigrants within it. When one reads these early commentaries on America by informed and literate observers one wonders if we have done right by our opportunities and circumstances.

Thomas Jefferson

We will not quote quite so extensively from the observations of the other observers, but an occasional passage in the original language seems to convey the spirit of the observations more accurately than paraphrase.

Thomas Jefferson is strong on agrarianism and makes a point that manufacture is necessary for European countries because their lands are largely locked up to the would-be farmer, but not so in America. The lands in the new continent are plentiful and call for cultivation by free men. He goes on to say

> . . . Those who labor on the earth are the chosen people of God, if ever he had a chosen people, whose breasts he had made his peculiar deposit for substantial and genuine virtue . . . Corruption of morals in the mass of cultivators is a phenomenon of which no age nor nation has furnished an example.

He argues that we should leave our workshops in Europe and that it is better to carry provisions and materials to them than to try to work them ourselves in the new America. He is downright pessimistic about urban developments:

> the mobs of great cities add just so much to the support of pure government, as sores do to the strength of the human body. It is the manners and spirit of a people which preserve a republic in vigor. A degeneracy in these is a cancer which soon eats to the heart of its laws and constitution.

The spirit of agrarianism has long been a value orientation in the American cultural dialogue. Until at least before World War I most 'respectable' American families had a farm somewhere in the extended family. Many people living in the small towns and villages across the continent had farms and also carried on trades or professions. The majority of the population moved from the farm to the city during the late nineteenth and early twentieth century. The movement is still continuing with a loss of single family farms amounting to hundreds each week. 'Farming as a way of life' has been the target of both critics and supporters and farm programs have been designed to support them, although the net effect is usually towards more consolidation and less individual family ownership and use.

The suburbanization of America that took place after World War II may, in a sense, be regarded as a back-to-the-land-movement. Though it seems a far cry from a small plot of grass with a house set down in the middle of it in a crowded suburb to a farm of several hundred acres or ranch of some thousand the underlying motivation may very well be much the same — the hunger for land, and the virtues presumably connected with the good earth.

Whatever one's sentiments about it, it seems clear that agriarianism had strong support in America. Thomas Jefferson is only one of its proponents. Two images seem to be in the American consciousness — one of them the ownership and cultivation of the land and the other the wilderness. As with many American value orientations there seems to be a point and a counter point. The dialogue is in part about the opposition. These oppositional tendencies may account for some of the peculiar dynamism of American culture.

Harriet Martineau

Harriet Martineau was a notable English reformer who travelled around the United States for two years beginning in 1834. Her observations were first published in 1837 in three volumes.

She makes some remarkable observations '. . . the worship of Opinion is, at this day, the established religion of the United States.' She even places the 'worship of Opinion' over the drive for wealth. She points out that where the will of the majority decides everything there is a strong need to belong to the majority. It takes an extremely strong will to be a member of the minority opposition.

She points out that this orientation towards conformity to the will of the majority is antagonistic to the individualism and freedom that Americans believe they have. In this way Martineau anticipated the anthropological interpretation that some would call 'structuralism' just applied in the paragraphs above about cultivated land and wilderness. The opposition between individualism and conformity that Martineau anticipates seems to be a persistent theme in the American cultural dialogue.

Alexis de Toqueville

When Alexis de Toqueville made his observations in 1831, the US was composed of twenty-four states and 13,000,000 people. He saw Americans as independent, resistant to authority, the children as pert and disrespectful, dedicated to an equable system of justice, but empty-headed, with a mortal dread of being different from the neighbors, and preoccupied with making money and obtaining material enjoyment.

He saw Americans as lonely, on their own two feet, and caring for little else than one's family and narrow group of friends. He saw them as consumed by a feverish drive for self-improvement, expressed in private exploitation of land, in commerce, and in work. He felt that Americans went about their business with a certain grimness — busy acquiring the good things of life that they then would presumably enjoy.

De Toqueville saw liberty as '. . . not the chief object of their desires; equality is their idol . . .'. This may in itself not sound contradictory but de Toqueville goes on to say that for Americans equality means conformity. And indeed he pictures the American as the very embodiment of conformity. Like Martineau, de Toqueville saw the American who was in the minority as 'not only mistrusting his strength, but even doubting of his right; and is very near acknowledging that he is in the wrong when the greater numbers of his countrymen assert that he is so.' He felt that actual freedom of opinion did not exist in America.

The opposition between individualism and conformity as framed by de Toqueville seems intense and pervasive in the American dialogue. We would tend to discount the extreme character of some of his criticisms were it not for the persistence of this opposition into politics and social relationships today. Even the attitudes expressed by students in our sample in response to questions concerning artists and intellectuals, to say nothing of college professors, would indicate that any form of deviation or even 'individuality' might be subject to criticism on the part of some. This seems to be a pivotal area for dialogue.

Baron J.A. Graf von Hübner

Baron Graf von Hübner was an Austrian ambassador to France and Italy who later became a member of the Austrian Reichsart and then took a 'ramble around the world' in 1871. Part of his ramble was through America. He comments,

> The first arrivals, the precursors of your actual greatness, those who sowed the seed, were discontented men. Intestine divisions and

religious persecutions had turned them from their homes and thrown them on your shores. They brought with them and implanted in the soil of their new country the principle for which they had suffered and fought — the authority of the individual. He who possesses it is free in the fullest acceptance of the term. And, as in that sense, you are all free, each of you is the equal of the other.

As all other observers in one way or another had done, Graf von Hübner recognized the strength of individuality as part of the American dialogue in this late nineteenth century context. He quite correctly pointed out that many, perhaps a majority, who immigrated to America came with great discontents and a vivid memory of persecution. Doubtless this has something to do with a noted American resentment of authority and a tendency to regard the individual as 'sacred' or 'supreme' — words used by students responding to the values projective technique.

But for Graf von Hübner the American brand of individualism was a mixed blessing. It resulted too often, in his view, in self-centered, self-aggrandizement. 'Rugged individualism' is what we might think of as being at the seat of his interpretation. This rugged individualism, he felt, made the coordination and productivity of the social whole difficult. There is certainly ample evidence to indicate that a marked degree of self-interest characterizes much of American behavior in business, the professions, and in government. Individualism does not mean the same thing in America that it means in Europe. The European concept is much closer to the notion of 'the character' or 'the original'. Individualism as a license for promoting self-interest is not seen so much as individualism in Europe but as a natural human tendency that has to be controlled by various sanctions of a moral as well as governmental origin. The American concept of individualism and of individuality seems to be a product of the opportunity afforded by the new land and the discontent with past experience that most immigrants to America have held, as Graf von Hübner and other observers have noted.

Frederick Jackson Turner

Frederick Jackson Turner first declared his 'frontier hypothesis' in the essay 'The Significance of the Frontier in American History' in 1893. He too is concerned with individualism, conformity and authority. He, like Graf von Hübner, also sees individualism in the American phrasing as both good and bad:

Individualism in America has allowed a laxity in regard to

governmental affairs which has rendered possible the spoils system and all the manifest evils that follow from a lack of a highly developed civic spirit. In this connection may be noted also the influence of frontier conditions in permitting lax business honor, inflated paper currency and wildcat banking.

But though individualism in the American framework had its disadvantages, there were more positive traits born of the frontier, as Turner interpreted it, that were very significant in the American socio-political and economic development.

> From the conditions of frontier life came intellectual traits of profound importance. . . . To the frontier the American intellect owes its striking characteristics. That coarseness and strength combined with acuteness and inquisitiveness; that practical, inventive turn of mind, quick to find expedience; that masterful grasp of material things, lacking in the artistic but powerful to effect great end; that restless, nervous energy; that dominant individualism, working for good and for evil, and with all that buoyancy and exuberance which comes with freedom — these are the traits of the frontier, or traits called out elsewhere because of the existence of the frontier.

This can be considered to be the 'frontier hypothesis' of Frederick Jackson Turner. Though it has been heavily critized by historians, it does not seem by any means to be entirely beside the point. Perhaps we are still acting as though the frontier in its traditional material sense still existed. But at the same time with the disappearance of this material frontier perhaps some of the characteristics, such as the 'masterful grasp of material things' likewise has diminished. This, at least, is part of the thesis presented by Marvin Harris in his book *Why Things Don't Work*. When one sees new commercial developments and new residential areas gobbling up good agricultural land without consequence for the environment or the future use of the land or when one learns of large corporations dumping poison into the ground and into the waterways, or clear-cutting redwood trees that were seedlings before Christ was born, one feels that individualism, self-interest, the drive for profit, as well as the 'coarseness and acuity' of the American character, do us all a disservice.

David Riesman

In 1951 the first book by David Riesman, *The Lonely Crowd* appeared, building upon previous work such as Turner's but adding something quite new. It is difficult to do justice to Riesman's work in a few short comments but we can point out that the central argument is something of the following.

Riesman posited an 'inner-directed' character type which he believed had psychological depth and historical relevance. The inner-directed person is oriented early in childhood towards very clear goals. He or she is headed in these directions by early socialization in a family that spends a lot of time educating their children and instilling moral values, work orientation, and success drive. Riesman regards this character type as 'gyroscopically-steered'. He thought of parents installing figurative gyroscopes in their children at an early age and this gyroscope keeps them on course for their whole lifetime.

He felt that the kind of society that this character type was best suited for was one in which production, discovery, and science were most important; 'Their preoccupation is to harness themselves to fulfilling the tasks of the expanding society which needs a large physical plant, extensive social organization, extensive military preparation.' This is a 'job-minded' society. People concentrate on necessary and rewarding tasks.

In contrast Riesman proposed another kind of character structure, the 'other-directed'. The inner-directed character type was conformity oriented in the sense that individuals so organized obeyed the built-in gyroscopic regulators. The other-directed character, however, has a new source of conformity. Riesman thought of the other-directed type as having a radar rather than a gyroscope installed. This kind of person is oriented early in life not to ancestors but to others, to peers. He regarded the schools of the 1950s, particularly the progressive schools, as places where the other-directed character type was encouraged. Teachers were interested, he said, in how well children got along with each other — even more than they were interested in how well they did with their school work.

Riesman does not overlook the fact that observers of the American scene such as those that we have cited often saw the American as other-directed. When Martineau talked about conformity this was the kind of character type that she was talking about. But Riesman was calling attention to the fact that we seem to be moving from a 'job-minded' society to a 'people-minded' society in which one's concern is no longer with the malleability of the material but with the malleability of the personnel.

In taking this stance he was contributing to the notion that social character matches socio-economic structure. From this point of view, though there might be many character types and individual personalities at any given time in a society, there would be broad tendencies towards one direction or another depending upon socio-economic development and change. Riesman seems to have been right about the movement from a job to a people-minded society and a movement from production to personnel.

It is said that we are becoming a 'service-oriented' society. We no longer produce goods but we can make arrangements of various kinds that promote distribution and consumption but also establish and maintain complex interpersonal relationships.

George Spindler developed and published in 1955 a theoretical model somewhat like David Riesman's from early work with the responses of Stanford University students to the values projective technique. On the basis of these data, he hypothesized that there was a 'traditional' and 'emergent' set of value orientations. The traditional value orientations resembled the inner-directed character type and conversely the emergent resembled the other-directed. He hypothesized that American society was moving from traditional to emergent. As we continued to collect data into the 1970s and 1980s, we could see that there was a cycling from traditional to emergent and back to traditional. We also began to see that both the traditional and emergent orientations were always present and probably had been from the very beginning.

We think that one of the basic dynamics of American society is that value orientations keep changing but the change is always in a cycle. There actually seem to be few radical breaks with the past in American cultural development.

David M. Potter

David Potter was a professor and chairman of the Department of History at Stanford University. He does not present big models like those of David Riesman or even like the Spindlers' traditional and emergent cycles, but rather tries to develop a complex configuration of attributes that he thinks are reasonably posited as the American character.

He refers, for example, to the intense preoccupation with our 'Americanism'. He traces this preoccupation to the fact that there is so much mixture of heritages, languages and religions among Americans and that only by accepting some obligation to 'be American' will we have anything at all in common.

As Potter goes further with his analysis he, too, copes with an observation that has been made many times before by observers of America since the beginning. He is concerned with the fact that so many have seen the American primarily as an individualist and at the same time as a conformist. He also links idealism with individualism and materialism with conformity. The emphasis on individual self-reliance he sees in much the same way that Frederick Jackson Turner saw it. He cites Thomas Jefferson and his exaltation of the independent farmer as the necessary component of the optimal society. The American frontier was basically an agricultural frontier and pioneers were therefore necessarily most often farmers even though hunters and explorers and fur traders had preceded them.

This concept of the individual, the self-reliant independent person able to strike out on his or her own (most usually his) Potter regarded as deep in the American self concept. But then he points out that egalitarianism and individualism, both important values, do not necessarily go together, as in fact Alexis de Toqueville had long ago noted. He saw the notion of equality for Americans as leading one to conformity and the love of well-being. In this framework, the individualist may be an idealist while the egalitarian may be a materialist and subject to mass-dominated conformity.

Conclusion

There seems always to be the problem of searching for grand models though, in justice to Professor Potter, it is true that he searches for configurative relationships rather than for absolute, block-like, characterizations.

As we previously noted, individuality may be interpreted to mean self-aggrandizement and equality may be interpreted to mean 'the same as' and therefore conformity-oriented. Capacities for highly individualistic, self-reliant, independent action and thinking seems to be very much present in America from the beginning, but at the same time, the other tendencies are certainly detectable. This is partly what we mean by a 'dialogue'. It is a dialogue about oppositions in pivotal areas such as the opposition between individualism and conformity, or the contradiction between equality meaning equality of opportunity and equality in the sense of attaining the same level of material prosperity in the same way as other 'successful' people.

These kinds of oppositions and their continuing unresolved tension in our national dialogue are what make American culture particularly interesting, and particularly dynamic. They are reflected in the responses to the values projective technique. We may think of the cycles apparent in the movement of value orientations and possibly even character types over time as being a kind of dynamic vacillation between opposite sides of contrastive and oppositional value orientations.

The oppositions extend beyond those mentioned to include freedom and constraint, cooperation and competition, sociability and individuality, as well as independence and conformity, Puritan morality and free love, materialism and altruism, hard work and 'getting by', and achievement and failure. We express this dialogue of oppositions in great and small institutions, political campaigns, expenditures of billions of dollars, schools and libraries, personnel management, business practices, sales pitches, production goals, foreign policy, etc. The dialogue of American culture has given meaning to our lives and actions as Americans and it has done so for more than 200 years since the Revolutionary period.

This dialogue has not gone unchanged and it is more preoccupied today with the degradation of our environment, our foreign policy or lack of it, the rights and justified expectations of members of minorities, with the meaning of religion in our lives, or the absence of it, with equality between the sexes and the contradictions between careers and child care, between careers and families, between peace and war, between men and women, with teen sex and pregnancy and the use of contraceptives, between 'pro-lifers' and 'pro-choicers' and a myriad of matters that have intruded upon our national consciousness in the past few decades and that were either absent or much more muted in our dialogue not long ago.

The central tension however, as we see it, is not so much between value orientations as between those who are carrying on the central dialogue and those who are excluded from it and who would like to be full participants. This is what we have tried to convey in our model of relationships in contemporary America between mainstream, referent ethniculture, and all minorities. The dialogue goes on and has gone on for a long time even though changing in form and emphasis with the times, but full participation in the dialogue has always been denied to some.

Women in the Cultural Dialogue

Before continuing to discuss the difficulties of transmitting this dialogue, we need to review the special case of women in the American cultural dialogue. How do women, the 'other' or the 'second' sex fit into the American cultural dialogue? The 'problem' of women may be considered a subset of the problem of diversity in American culture. Anthropologists have until recently neglected women in their research. Because a majority of anthropologists have been males it is not surprising that they have attended to the highly visible public roles played by males in most societies. In the classic analyses of American culture by sociologists and historians, it has been assumed that since American men have been dominant status-wise, the characteristics of American men are the characteristics of all American people, including women. In his frontier hypothesis, Turner was referring only to male values. Riesman's concept of a shift from inner- to other-orientation is quite inapplicable to women, who have always been other-oriented to children and family. At best, the women's world is difficult for a male to research. Now that female anthropologists are focusing on women in crosscultural studies and therefore calling attention to the infrastructures of society instrumented mainly by women, we can expect to eventually reexamine role relationships in American society from a crosscultural viewpoint. Jane Collier, for example, views women as political strategies who use resources available to them in support of interests often opposed to those of men. Women's strategies, she claims, are important components of the processes by which social life proceeds. This kind of approach could well be the focus of some anthropological work on American women, particularly because they have, in part, moved out of infrastructural roles.

Florence Kluckhohn, a sociologist with strong anthropological leanings, has presented one of the few organized macro models of differences in male and female roles in mainstream American culture. Using her 'value orientation' schema, she showed that women's roles historically have expressed 'variant' rather than 'dominant' values in American culture. She posited that individualism — with man as autonomous free agent — was a dominant male value, while women as wives and mothers were oriented toward group goals. Where the valued personality type for males was the 'person of action', the 'doing personality', for women it was the philanthropist type, dedicated to community improvements and family morality. And while the time orientation for males has been the future, for practical reasons it has been the present for women. Some such form of cultural analysis, with appropriate modification, might be applicable to the contemporary scene.

Women have not been shut out of the dialogue, for they have created a significant part of it in their roles within the infrastructure, and they have historically carried on the dialogue within civic and domestic contexts. However, the phrasing of the dialogue in the interpretive literature is most always on classic male terms. There is a strong sexist component in all of the observers' comments on the American scene. It is almost as if women did not exist and that the new continent had been peopled exclusively by males. That is the reason why in Figure 3.2 we put women outside the mainstream culture circle. This positioning is problematic but it calls attention to the fact that women are *in* but not *of* the expressed cultural dialogue.

Notes

Jean de Crevecoeur, Thomas Jefferson, Harriet Martineau, Alexis de Toqueville, Baron J. A. Graf von Hübner, and Frederick Jackson Turner, all early observers of the American scene, are represented selectively in Rapson (1967). Marvin Harris (1986) and David Riesman (1951) produce analyses related to Turner's. In 1955 G. Spindler published a summary of the results produced by the Values Projective Technique applied to education in the United States. David Potter (1954) faced the problem of the oppositions between independence and conformity in the American character — a problem encountered in various forms by most of the other observers. Women occupy a special place in the American cultural dialogues, as Jane Collier (1974), Florence Kluckhohn (1951), and Simone de Beauvoir (1953) point out.

Chapter 5

Schooling in the American Cultural Dialogue

Counseling for Success and Failure

The scene is the eighth grade room in Fairmount School in a coastal California community. There is a middle-aged woman standing in front of the room telling the children about their choices as they enter high school. There are thirty-five children in the room. About 50 per cent appear to be Mexican American. Later I discover that the California mental maturity test, elementary form, indicates a range of seventy-five to 114. The mean is ninety-seven. This is what is described as a 'middle range' group.

The counselor says, 'You must be a good citizen, or they won't accept you. You can have two failures but not three. Now what do you need to get into junior college?' (Students raise their hands and repeat answers they have previously been given.) 'What do you need to get into San Jacinto State College?' (same response) 'Now what do you need to get into the University of California? Now you ask me questions, if there are any . . . are there any? We've talked about this a lot here, but you haven't had a chance to ask many questions. Are there any?' (a three second pause, no questions) Now I want all of you to come and see me — bring this slip. If you forget it, make another. You can remember what's on it. Now you may ask, when can we come to see you? Well, I'll be there at nine o'clock, ten o'clock, and later. You can get a pass from me. Or you can come after school, just any night you want to.'

The counselor continues with the task for that hour. She starts arranging some program choices for next year on the board. She writes down six numerals and puts 'P.E.' after number one, 'English' after number two and 'Social Studies' after number three and then turns to the class, 'Now you have to decide whether you want to take Algebra or not. You have to take Math all the way through high school, if you want to be an engineer. Now if you've gotten B's and C's all the way through eighth grade what are your chances of doing well in ninth grade algebra?' (Children groan and mutter) 'Not so good, that's right!'

The teacher continues, 'So what can you do?' (Someone says, 'Well, try to raise your grade.') 'Yes, that's one thing you can do.' (Someone else says, 'work harder.') 'Yes, that's another thing you can do. But what else?' (silence) 'Well do like I did, when I wanted to be an opera singer, but found I couldn't sing . . . what did I do?' (Children say various things but among them, 'you changed your plans.') 'That's right! I changed my plans!'

'How many here speak Spanish?' (Six of the seventeen who may speak Spanish raise their hand.) 'It will help you if you do. But you have to realize that there is some work to do. It is good if you speak Spanish if you want to go to college and need a language.'

'You can't take Spanish and general business. No, they come on the same period. Now, one of the things is to be neat, and orderly. If you aren't good at that it might be hard for you until you've learned to do it better.'

'Now we come to mechanical drawing. This is exclusively a boys' class, but I don't know why some girls couldn't take it if they wanted to. But only boys take it.'

'Now let's look at agriculture as a possibility. This is also a boy's subject. You have to keep an animal of some kind. And you will be taken to a ranch.'

'Now about home making. This is just for girls.'

'Now when you come to see me, if I tell you to take general business instead of Spanish it should be understood that you don't have to take it. You can do just as you wish. But it means that I think you would do better in general business.'

'Now about dramatics — you will learn to stand before a group, speak distinctly, and enunciate clearly. And once or twice a year you will get to put on a play.'

'Now you know there is something called girls' shop. There you learn to fix a wire if you're ironing and it breaks.'

'Now when you pass the typing class it looks interesting doesn't it? But do you know that there aren't any letters on those keyboards? You have to watch a chart at the front of the room, and if you look at the keyboard you fail!'

The bell rings and the children begin to get restless and prepare to go. The counselor says, 'Just a moment now. Are there any questions? No? Well, all right, then you may go.'

After the observation the counselor talked with the observer. 'This is a passive group. There's no spark in there. The better groups get quite excited about this. Of course most of the groups are college preparatory.' (The observer asks how many would be college preparatory in this group.) 'Only about three or four, maybe none of this group that you saw today will go on to college. Now I hope you understand that these are the scum of the middle group. They are not as good a group to observe as the one you were going to come to see on Thursday as originally planned. We thought of putting them in various classes but felt it was a shame to spoil the good groups.'

This counseling session took place in the early 1950s and one is inclined to say that it could not happen today. Our observations of schools in America, however, suggest that though the specific forms may have changed the spirit is often there. It is not that teachers or counselors intentionally disadvantage children or purposefully advantage children, as most are well-intentioned and of good heart. But the culture of the school, fitting the culture of our larger society and its dialogue, does separate out children for success and failure. These children were separated this way and they are now a parental generation. We are preoccupied with failure. As Ray McDermott has tellingly pointed out, failure is waiting for every child, but some children more than others, in every classroom and school in America. The failure or the learning disability is there before the child arrives. Given this structure, the counselor, or the teacher, has the task of finding children to fit the structure.

What this counseling session did was to open some gates for some children who, it was thought, were college bound, and closed gates for others. One would think there would be other gates opened if the college preparatory gate was closed but they were not. Some children were informed again and again that there really wasn't much hope for them, and most of those children were of Mexican descent. Even typing was too hard and too threatening as the counselor described it.

Now we will move on to a different kind of situation, a fifth grade classroom in another West coast school taught by a young man who is regarded within the school system as an individual of great promise.

A Fifth Grade Classroom and Teacher

Our purpose in this chapter is to analyze how the school may act as a cultural transmitter and the teacher as a cultural mediator. Another way of saying this is to ask how the school selects children to participate in the American dialogue in different ways. Some children will be incorporated in the mainstream dialogue. Others will be left out of the mainstream dialogue but will be encouraged to make a positive adaptation with it. Yet others will, in effect, be discarded, left so far outside of the center there is little hope for them to move into it.

How can this happen in one classroom of thirty-seven children and one teacher? The finishing touches are not put on the process until later in one's school career and after many other teachers and counselors have been encountered. Some children, perhaps as many as 25 per cent in the nation's schools as a whole, drop out before the second year of high school. The proportion is much higher in some urban school districts. The combination of their experience in their home and community with the experience in the school has by then predestined them for marginality. But other children are promoted and encouraged in manifold ways.

Does this mean that the teacher is overtly prejudiced towards some children? Does it mean that the teacher is racist? In this case and in most of the classrooms that we have visited in America teachers are neither of those things. The teacher we studied in particular, a young man of twenty-six with three years of teaching experience, was determined to give every child in his classroom a fair chance. He believed that he was 'fair and just to all of the children', that he was 'fair in all decisions regarding children', that he was 'easy for children to approach with their problems'. We know his self-perceptions because we asked him to rate himself in a number of behavior areas that we considered to be relevant to our analysis of his classroom interaction and his philosophy of teaching. The graph presenting his self rating is presented in Figure 5.1. If rank three is 'about like most other teachers' and rank five is 'definitely better than most teachers' you can see that he thinks well of himself as a teacher.

This teacher rates himself above this average rating on all counts excepting 'discipline of the class', 'assisting students in planning' and 'students free to work'. Actually his classroom was the most disciplined of those that we visited in his school and he is right in that students were not as free to work on their own projects as in some classes. He felt that the discipline in many other classrooms was not as strict as it should be and that his should be better.

He seemed to be a little too self-critical in his rating of assisting students in planning, but on most dimensions of the teaching role he rates himself as somewhat better than most teachers or definitely superior to most other teachers. It is particularly notable that he rates himself as superior on 'fair in decisions concerning students' and 'understanding student problems'. He rates himself as 'somewhat' better than most teachers in fairness of grading, sympathy for students and students sharing decisions. These self-ratings are all directly relevant to the evaluation of equity in his classroom.

We asked all of the administrators and counselors who had any direct knowledge of his operation as a teacher to also rate him on the same scales. These included the principal and vice principal, all of the special services people who visited his classroom and all of the people in the superintendent's office, including the superintendent himself.

Understand Student Problems	Students Free to Work	Students Share Decisions	Personal Appearance	General Teaching Ability	Ability to Explain Clearly	Assist Students in Planning	Value of Topics	Fair in Decisions re: Students	Sympathetic to Students	Students Like Subject	Discipline of Class	Amount Students Learning	Students Like Personality	Fairness of Grading	Knowledge of Subject

5

4

3

2

1

Figure 5.1 Teacher's Rating of Self

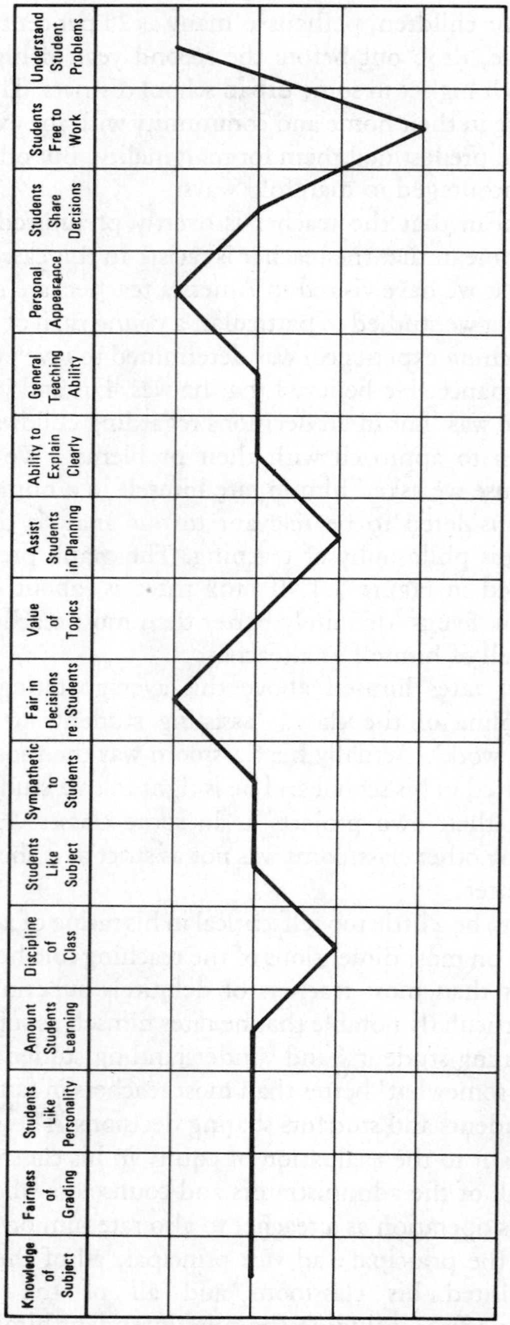

Source: G. and L. Spindler.

Figure 5.2 Administrator Rating of Teacher and Teacher's Estimate of Administrator Rating

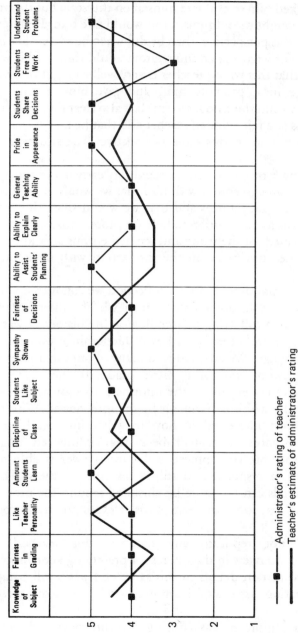

Administrator's rating of teacher
Teacher's estimate of administrator's rating

Source: G. and L. Spindler.

The administrators rate him higher than he rates himself (see Figure 5.2). There are no behavorial areas where he drops below the presumed average for other teachers.

We also asked him to evaluate himself on this scale but this time to rate himself as he thought the administrators would rate him. He rates himself a little higher, in this perspective, than he did when he was evaluating himself without regard for what the administrators would think of his work.

It is clear that this young teacher is very well thought of by the people who will judge him, promote him, and give him security within the profession and within the school system. It is also clear that he is confident of his effectiveness as a fair-minded teacher and that he knows that others who evaluate him see him in this same perspective. The situation seems very positive.

These rating forms were administered very early in our contact with this teacher. We had an agreement with him that we would study his classroom for a period of several months and that we would share the results of our study with him as a contribution to his own professional self-improvement. He had volunteered for the study and seemed enthusiastic about it and the reinforcement he anticipated in the interaction with us as unprejudiced observers.

After this initial period of data collection we conducted what we have called the 'expressive autobiographic interview'. This interview procedure is quite different than collecting a chronological life history. It was developed by Louise Spindler in her early work with Menominee women adapting to rapid cultural change. We adapted it to many of our other research projects including the work with this fifth grade teacher. The expressive autobiographic interview allows the informant to start wherever he or she wishes but usually within a frame set by the interviewer. With teachers we were usually most interested in how they got into teaching and what formative experiences there had been that influenced them towards teaching. As the interview proceeds the interviewer is able to reinforce certain avenues of response and subtly discourage others. The autobiographical materials can therefore be clustered around the promontories of experience and reaction that seem most relevant to the purposes of the research.

We will not replicate any part of this teacher's expressive autobiographic interview in the interest of preserving anonymity. (We have already cloaked certain details to this same end.) We will paraphrase and comment on various aspects of the interview relevant to our presentation in this chapter.

He seemed quite at ease during the interview and impressed the interviewer as 'uncomplicated' in the sense that he was pleasant, seemingly relaxed, but did not have a strong impact upon the observer. He seemed to accept himself, his role, the situation, and most parts of the transaction, without much attempt at manipulation.

The first question directed at him was 'I just want to get some understanding of your personal experience and background in relationship to teaching. We might start right there with teaching. How did you happen to go into teaching?' His answer was that he was really influenced by his mother who had been a music teacher and by his sister who also taught in grade school for a while. He had been in the army during the Korean War and wanted to develop a profession after he was discharged and felt that it was most definitely due to the influence of his mother and sister that he went back to school with the aim of becoming a teacher. He made it clear that he regarded teaching in the elementary school as a stepping-stone to administration and was in fact working for his administrative credential at a West Coast university during summers and other released time. He expected to obtain the credential and the Master of Arts degree within two or three years and by that time have an administrative post, probably as principal of an elementary school. He thought of himself as ultimately destined for the superintendency.

Another question was 'Let's go back to before college. What was your family like?' He indicated that they had always gotten along very well in his family and then spoke of his mother and sister and how his sister had played at a number of recitals and that both his mother and sister were very talented on the piano. In the course of the interview he did not bring up his father spontaneously. He responded to a direct question about him that he was a manager for a large retail organization.

He went on to say that what they really enjoyed doing the most was driving up to their summer home in the mountains and that he would go with his mother and sister for a month or two every summer. His father would come up occasionally on weekends. The park where the summer home was located was maintained by the Masonic Lodge.

When asked more about his father he indicated that his father was very active in various civic organizations such as the American Legion, the Masonic Lodge, the Elks, and the Kiwanis. Both of his parents also went to the Methodist Church, attending frequently but not with absolute regularity. He himself attended church only infrequently.

Other questions had to do with the kind of neighborhood he was born into and any changes in residence that he had experienced with his parents. He indicated that there had been a more or less consistent progression towards bigger and better homes but that he has never lived in anything but a good neighborhood, as he put it.

When asked about his use of spare time he indicated that he read professional journals (*National Education Association Journal* and the *California Teachers' Association Journal*) but that he also liked to read the local community newspaper and the *Saturday Evening Post*. For recreation he liked going to the beach and spending the day relaxing best.

There are many many details and events that this summary does not include, but it is apparent from his expressive autobiographic interview that he is mainsteam and middle class. He probably qualifies as referent ethniclass because he is Anglo-Saxon Protestant. His father's status as a manager for a large scale retail organization would class the family economically and professionally in the upper-middle class. His own position as an aspiring-to-be school administrator does not by itself place him in this category, but it is clear that his socioeconomic status and cultural position are at least squarely within the middle class mainstream and that his origins are upper middle class. He, himself, seems to be striving for this status and to match his father's success.

The question that we were interested in answering as we proceeded with the case study was in what ways his cultural background affected his interaction with the children in his classroom. The answer to this question required a great deal of observation and further interviewing. The mass of data is far beyond what we can even sample in this chapter. We will select out only a few highlights.

We observed his movements about the classroom and found that they took him to only certain parts of the room and near certain children on a regular basis. Furthermore, he eye-engaged, touched, and interacted only with certain children and rarely or not at all with others. He nodded, smiled, and appeared to approve as certain children performed before the class, as in 'sharing' — a period when children told about their weekends or other special experiences. He was never observed being mean or overtly hostile in behavior, facial expression or comment to any of the children.

We discovered that children seemed to be grouped by socioeconomic status and ethnicity. The explicit basis for the grouping, the teacher told us, was reading ability. About one-third of the class of thirty-seven were Mexican-American, Black, or Portuguese and these children were also of low socioeconomic status.

We interviewed each child for about twenty minutes and later administered a rating scale questionnaire to them concerning the teacher's behavior and the classroom in general. From the interviews plus school records and a house-by-house neighborhood and district evaluation we were able to determine socioeconomic status and ethnicity as well as family culture with a high degree of reliability.

When the children rated the teacher on some fifty points on the rating scale questionnaire we got a surprise. The children rated him below the average for other teachers they had had on five specific points. All five of the ratings had to do with his accessibility and what was perceived as selective interaction with some children. The lower socioeconomic status and non-mainstream children rated him as difficult to take their problems to, hard to get help from and not fair in his decisions concerning them. They also charged him with having favorites with whom he was always interacting.

Figure 5.3   Students' Evaluation of Teacher

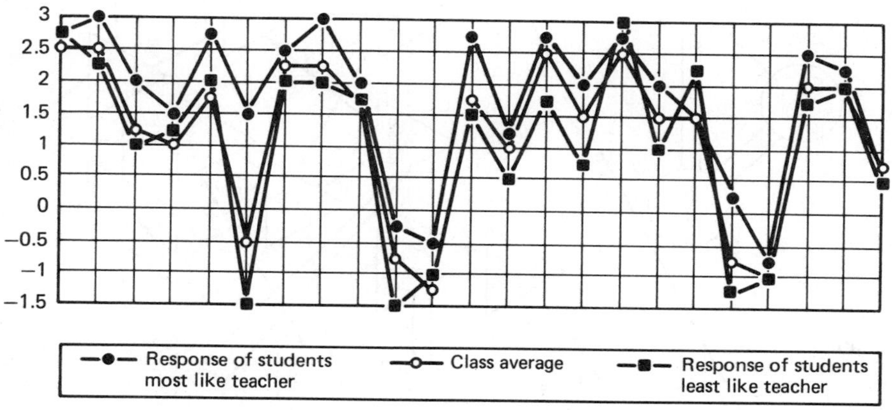

—●— Response of students most like teacher   —○— Class average   —■— Response of students least like teacher

Source: G. and L. Spindler.

These ratings by the children supported some of our observations of his classroom behavior. It appeared that a pattern of selective interaction was emerging quite clearly in our data. The question then became, what was the nature of this interaction?

Our sociometric data served us well at this point. We collected several forms of ratings from the children themselves concerning interaction in the classroom, particularly among peers, and checked them against our own observations. We also asked the teacher to estimate and describe each child's interaction with his or her peers and then matched his perceptions of these relationships with those that we collected from the children. We found that the teacher was biased in his perception of relationships. The bias was consistently in the direction of positive appraisals for upper status and mainstream children. He was as consistently *negative* in his appraisal of relationships for non-mainstream children as he was positive for the others.

Some examples will clarify. If we take 'Mary' for example. He described Mary as 'my favorite pupil, a great sense of humor, everyone likes and respects her a great deal, she is a born leader!' The children leave her fairly

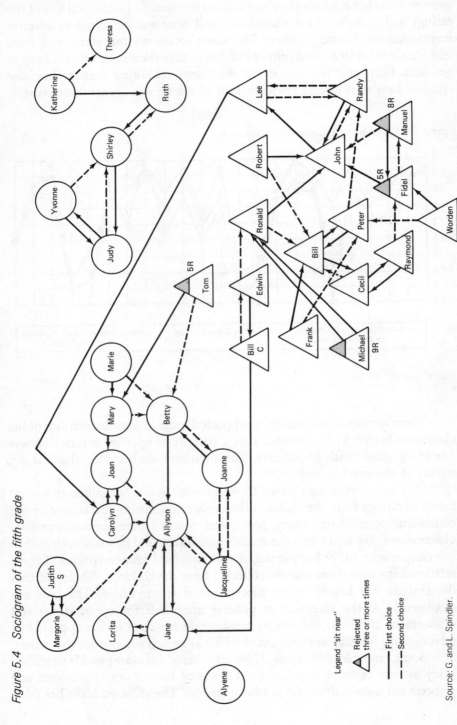

Figure 5.4 Sociogram of the fifth grade

Legend "sit near"
△ Rejected three or more times
—— First choice
---- Second choice

Source: G. and L. Spindler.

isolated. On the sociogram (Figure 5.4) constructed from a proximity rating by each child of his or her choices in the group, Mary is chosen by two children who are themselves entirely isolated, and her own first choices are not reciprocated.

Who is Mary? Her father is the owner of a string of retail clothing stores. The family income places them well into referent class position and they qualify in other respects — they are Anglo-Saxon, North European Protestant. Mary takes vacations with her family in Hawaii, Alaska, and Europe. The teacher enjoys her reports of these trips during the sharing period. Mary is a well dressed and attractive child. She speaks well and responds to the teacher's questions and participates in a lively manner in the discussions.

Another one of the teacher's favorites is a boy named 'Tom'. On the same sociogram that Mary appears, Tom is not chosen by anyone and is rejected five times. He chooses Mary. He is designated as someone 'I would not like to six next to' by five children.

The teacher describes Tom as 'a real go-getter, one of the most magnetic personalities of any young child I have ever known. He has a very warm personality and gets along well with anyone, anywhere. He is truthful, sincere, and has a wonderful sense of humor.'

During the sharing periods Tom gets up with a little black satchel filled with samples from one of his father's several retail drug stores. He goes into his sales pitch and, by the end of his time, has collected nickels and dimes from the children in exchange for the sample tubes of toothpaste, hair oil, perfume and powder, and various other odds and ends that he has brought to school to 'share'. The children appreciate the bargain but they do not appreciate Tom.

Tom's background is very much like that of Mary's. His family is well-to-do and his ethnic and cultural position, like hers, places him in the referent upper-middle class mainstream.

There are several other instances of this kind, but the point should be clear by now. This teacher quite unconsciously selected out children for approval and reinforcement that had backgrounds much like his and represented his aspirations towards success. He was not, as we have said, actively prejudicial in his relationships with children who did not fit into this category. He was essentially a kind and very well-meaning person. But it is clear that he gave further impetus toward achievement and success on mainstream terms to some children and unintenionally denied it to others. Of course some of the 'others' survived despite his inattention and when they showed strong interest in learning he would help them. The motivation had to come from them, however.

This configuration is all the more remarkable when we remember that this teacher professed an ideology of fairness and equity. He had strong ideological commitments, but his selective and unintentionally prejudicial behavior in the classroom belied his professed ideology.

When we arrived at the point where our contractual relationship called for the sharing of our research findings, our relationship with the teacher suddenly becamed quite strained. When we showed him the results of our observations, the application of rating scales, our interviews, and sociometric data, and especially when we matched his perceptions against those of the children, he denied, at first, that it could be true. In fact, he became very angry and left the room, slamming the door. However, we were able to reestablish a working relationship and went through the body of data that we had collected and discussed their possible meaning. He gradually, if albeit reluctantly, came to accept most of the material. He kept saying 'I can't believe that I did that, I can't believe that I didn't see that happening'.

We pointed out to him his own cultural background and the way in which it appeared to have affected his perceptions of interaction with children in his classroom. This was hard for him to accept at first, but it was certainly much easier than if we have been concerned with a personality problem. We attempted to steer clear of psychological involvements as much as possible and focus almost entirely upon the cultural process.

We eventually came to call this relationship 'cultural therapy'. This may be an unfortunate term in that it implies that there was an illness that could be corrected by therapy. In a sense this was true, though this teacher and many others with whom we worked were not ill people; there was a cultural relationship that determined to what degree and in what ways children were caught up in the classroom interaction and ultimately, we believed, in the American cultural dialogue. This relationship was advantageous to some children and disadvantageous to others. Particularly when there was such an obvious mismatch between the teacher's beliefs in what he or she was doing, and what was actually transpiring, the term 'therapy' seemed appropriate.

It should be clear that we are not espousing a simple 'culture conflict' theory. We are saying that one's cultural background significantly influences what one will value, disvalue, and ignore. This teacher's problem was not so much disvaluing as ignoring. He simply did not interact in the same way or with the same intensity with children who did not match his own cultural experience and background. This process of selecting out certain children and certain behaviors for approval and reinforcement, and ignoring others, is potentially as damaging as the exercise of overt prejudice and hostility towards certain children. The cultural therapy in this teacher's case consisted of bringing him to realize that his own declared commitments were not being implemented in the classroom due to a cultural bias of which he was largely unaware. We feel that such sensitivity training should be incorporated in teacher training programs as well as in in-service work of the kind that we were doing. Each teacher is somewhat unique, but all teachers, as cultural transmitters, are subject to some of these same hazards.

Conclusion

In the case of the eighth grade counselor there is blatant prejudice and both positive and negative selection. As a gate keeper, this counselor had more power than she realized. She was sending some children on to glory with her blessing and condemning others to perdition with her curses. This statement is a little over-dramatic but it does fit the case. We did not find many other counselors so prejudiced and so damaging but we found elements of this kind among many, if not most, of the ones that we observed in action during five years of intermittent work in the schools.

When we did a careful study of academic achievement and California Mental Maturity (CMM) test scores for Mexican-American children in one West Coast school district, we found that the longer the children stayed in school, the more they dropped in academic performance in relation to expected performance at the appropriate grade level and that their CMM scores declined — not only in the verbal portion of the test scores but in the non-verbal portion. It is correct to say that the longer these children stayed in school, the lower their relative academic performance and the lower their intelligence quotient (as measured by this particular test). This is what alienation does: it dulls and destroys abilities and potentialities.

By the time this counselor had the power of channeling and gate-keeping over the children in the observed eighth grade group, they had already had enough experience to know where they belonged and where they were probably going to go. All she did was reinforce their expectations. The school is indeed a factory for both failure and success.

And who was this counselor? She was a woman in her sixties not far from retirement who had served in the school district faithfully for many years and was well regarded by the administration and by her peers. She was regarded as a 'little old fashioned' but certainly competent and sympathetic to children. She was the daughter of an Italian immigrant who had worked his life out as an intermittent day laborer. She had known poverty and had herself climbed the ladder to middle class status through her education and by becoming a teacher, then a counselor. One would think this kind of experience would lead her to a particularly effective relationship with non-mainstream children, as sometimes happens. Just as often however, it does not happen because the person is compensating for his or her past experience. What this counselor wanted to do was to expurgate those qualities that led children, as she perceived them, to failure. In expurgating these qualities she also expurgated the children, but to her this seemed to be a necessary cost. When individual Mexican-American children showed special motivation or ability she would work with them. But she regarded the situation for most of them as hopeless.

The fifth grade teacher had much the same effect on children as the counselor but since he came from quite a different place culturally, he exercised his biases differently. He did not actively select children for failure, but he did actively select children for success. He selected those children for success who were already successful and like himself culturally. This positive pattern of interaction gave both him and the children that he was positive about a very good feeling. He left other children with a residue of disappointment and negativism. He was such a 'nice' teacher that this negativism did not show up in hostile behavior in the classroom. But the negativism was continuously reinforced by every positive move he made towards his favorites. By the time these children reach the eighth grade they will have been selected out for success and failure, and then they will meet another cultural agent who will put the finishing touches on their finishing.

American culture is a process. It is not only a process of opposition, accommodation, and resolution, but also of selection, reinforcement, and of success and failure. In an achievement-oriented culture where one of the salient and desired features of the mainstream culture is personal achievement and success, failure is all the more poignant. Children do not like to fail anymore than do adults. Children spend a great deal of their time avoiding failure — if not by achievement then by not engaging. Dropping-out begins early, but it is not a personal predisposition. It is a product of the interaction between people, institutions, and cultural patterns.

Notes

The transmission of culture in the school has been one of our professional preoccupations; see Spindler (1959), (1987). Ray McDermott discusses the failure waiting for every child in 'Making Dropouts,' his discussant remarks in the report of the first centennial conference at Stanford University on children at risk (H. Trueba, G. and L. Spindler, 1989) and in a related paper on competition (with S. Goldman, 1987). See also the same volume for papers and discussions of dropping out of school. The 'cultural therapy' for the fifth grade teacher is discussed in G. and L. Spindler (1989). The expressive autobiographic interview technique is discussed briefly by Louise Spindler in G. and L. Spindler (1971).

Chapter 6

Conflict and Accommodation of Mainstream and Minority Values

We have tried to develop a coherent model of what we think of as the central dynamics of the American cultural dialogue, put it in some historical perspective and selectively describe some aspects of its transmission. In this chapter we will discuss an example of conflict and accommodation between minorities and the mainstream. We have chosen a Native American case because the forms of conflict and accommodation characteristic of mainstream/Native American relations, though extreme, will illuminate some features common to all. Further, this exercise will put mainstream value orientations and the dialogue surrounding them into sharper perspective.

In our long term study of the Menominee of north central Wisconsin, we were fortunate to interact with persons representing a range of sociocultural adaptations from what we termed 'native oriented' or traditional, to people who appeared, behaviorally, to be wholly mainstream. The native-oriented group, during the time of our most intensive field work (1950–69), lived well off the highways and in the forest, and carried on traditional rituals such as the Medicine Lodge and the Dream Dance, as well as a number of minor rituals that were carried on each week rather than seasonally. The people in this group lived in modified wigwams, shacks, log cabins and quonset-type habitations, earned their living by working intermittently in the lumber industry, but more often by picking crops such as cherries, potatoes, and strawberries and by hunting, fishing and gathering. Though their culture was certainly not unchanged, it was a good representation of the traditional Menominee and central Algonkian culture type that had dominated the area for hundreds of years.

It was not until we had done fieldwork with this group for several seasons that we realized that most of the people under sixty have been away from the reservation community, going to school and working, and knew a lot about mainstream culture. In fact, they knew too much, for they had made the decision to come back and 'be Indian'. They were self-conscious and purposeful about their choice and were committed to maintaining as much of the recognizable traditional culture as possible. We called this behavior 'Reaffirmative Adaptation' because the traditional culture was not simply surviving, it was being revitalized and reaffirmed.

The Confrontation

The relationship with the mainstream culture as the members of the native-oriented group had experienced it was not simply one of conflict in the passive sense, but one of confrontation. The way of life of the traditional Menominee and the way of life of the mainstream are irreconcilably opposed. To express this in the most efficient form we provide Figure 6.1. On the left side are pivotal areas of mainstream culture and on the right side these same areas are interpreted from the traditional Menominee point of view.

Figure 6.1 The Confrontation

AMERICAN MAINSTREAM	TRADITIONAL MENOMINEE
material power	spiritual power
individualism	autonomy
achievement orientation	achievement only in sacred power
aggressive	latescent (waiting expectantly)
expressive modes	stoic (controlled)
competitive	noncompetitive
humans control and change nature	humans live in nature
future oriented	present oriented
simple religious beliefs	complex religious beliefs
complex technology	simple technology but highly adaptive to the environment
sex repressive (?)	sex repressive

Source: G. and L. Spindler.

Power

The opposed cultural orientations listed require further explanation. Power, for the traditional Menominee, was spiritual and gained by fasting, humility, and by observing the proper rituals in the right frame of mind. Without spiritual power, from the Menominee point of view, there could be no material power. One was able to partake of the power suffusing the universe by the correct ritual procedures, but the proper state of mind always had to go along with the ritual.

At puberty both boys and girls were given from time to time, a choice at breakfast between charcoal and food. If they chose the charcoal they would enter into a period of fasting. This might occur a number of times. At the Big Fast they would be isolated and without food or water or the comfort of human companionship for days. During this time a spiritual entity would appear, such as the Golden Eagle or White Bear, and take the faster upon his back to show him or her the sacred places in the Menominee territory. This spiritual entity, which usually represented an important animal spirit in the Menominee pantheon, would impart some information, though frequently in the form of metaphors or stories that required interpretation. After the initiate returned to ordinary life he or she would go to a 'clairvoyant', one of several forms of shamans, and receive instruction and interpretation giving detailed meaning to the experience. This ritual was one of the major routes to power. There were, however, other ways of obtaining power. Some consisted of nothing more than a short ritual to honor a spiritual entity that had been inherited from an ancestor. One of our informants, for example, would put a small amount of whiskey in a bowl, and engage in a ritual which involved lapping up the whiskey and upturning the bowl with his head as a buffalo might, and then smoking a special pipe and making a tobacco sacrifice. By doing this he renewed the power of the buffalo 'guardian spirit' that had been given to him by his grandfather. Whatever it was that happened, or however one obtained this kind of power, it was a determining influence in one's life course. Without it one was weak, incapable of important deeds, even helpless.

Individualism / Autonomy

If we look at the concept of individualism we find a dramatic difference between mainstream American and the traditional Menominee point of view. To the mainstreamer, the individual is the unit of social and moral action, served by the social and political structure. From the traditional Menominee point of view, individualism in this particular sense did not exist. Rather, the *person* was the ideal. The two concepts do overlap, but where American individualism often results in a kind of conformity to the expectations of others and is subject to control by hierarchical authority, Menominee autonomy does not. The autonomous individual was responsible to no one and was responsible for all of his or her own decisions. Even a child of 5 or 6 years of age was regarded as having the ability to decide what he or she wanted. If, for instance, a parent had made an elaborate dancing costume for a young child and the child were to sell it to a tourist for a few dollars, the child might complain that there was no costume when it came time to dance again. The parent would then say, without recrimination in manner or voice, 'You sold it to that man'. It was simply a statement of fact and with the assumption that if the child chose to sell it, then the consequences of that action were not something that anyone else could control.

Traditional Menominee persons are so autonomous that there can be no concept of 'chief', a concept which was a construct of Euro-American cultural perceptions anyway. Within the traditional framework, the only way that a group can be brought together in decision-making is through unanimous and unpressured consent. We saw many instances of this during our field work. It took us a long time to understand that no one could represent another person and that no one had authority over another person — not even parents over children.

Achievement

Achievement orientation differs between the mainstream and the traditional Menominee in that for the Menominee there was achievement only through spiritual power. For the mainstreamer achievement is through hard work, personal endeavor, and aggressive manipulation of circumstances. From the Menominee point of view this kind of behavior is likely to get one bewitched. If anyone does markedly better than other people existing under the same conditions, one is subject to witchcraft, because others think that one is using some exceptional and perhaps black power to achieve this success. A traditional Menominee person is careful not to stand out in this way. To do so is regarded as 'biting one's own tail'.

Aggression/Latescence

Aggression is controlled and displaced in mainstream American culture and it is true that highly aggressive people are likely to get socially 'witched'. However, controlled aggression is necessary for the achievement of individualistic goals in a competitive society. Again, from the traditional Menominee point of view, this use of aggression is misplaced. The proper frame of mind is something we came to term *latescent*. *Latescence* is a form of expectant waiting that is likely to be interpreted by mainstreamers as a kind of passive dependency. This is not correct, however, because the expectant waiting requires great self-control and at times, endurance.

One time, when the authors returned from the 'outside world' to rejoin the traditional Menominee group, we went back to where the people lived in the forest and found that all of the houses were vacant. It was apparent that the people had gone to work a crop or perhaps to a Medicine Lodge ceremony somewhere else. Finally, however, we found one house that appeared to be occupied. We drove into the yard, and after a decent interval, stepped out of the car and went to the door. After we had sat on the door stoop for a while, as good manners in the traditional group require, we called the name of the woman we knew should be inside, and she responded. We went in to find her sitting in a chair holding a baby. We saw also that another child was lying on a nearby couch. We talked for a while about ordinary things — where we had been and what had happened while we were gone and where everybody was. But we knew that there was something wrong. It turned out that she had been left behind and her husband had temporarily deserted her, as he sometimes did. She gave birth to the baby by herself. Her older son was ill with a fever, and there was neither food nor money in the house. It was a situation that would have called for hysteria among most middle class mainstream Americans. She was very controlled and appeared quite normal to superficial examination. Of course, we took action, got groceries, gave the boy some aspirin, helped out as best we could and arranged for a visit from the nurse from reservation headquarters. We asked our friend how she felt during this period of what we thought of as a crisis and she said 'I knew something would happen, somebody would come and I just had to wait. And then you came.' This is an example of latescence.

Expressive / Stoic

Being expressive as opposed to being 'stoic' is very much like the contrast between being aggressive and being latescent. The traditional Menominee express the full range of emotions, but to the outsider this expression seems muted. Their emotional displays are carefully controlled and the evidence from projective tests that we collected from the members of this group indicates that this control goes quite deep. In a culture where sorcery is an ever-present threat, the control of emotional expression is extremely important. Beyond this there is also the fact that emotional displays and in fact any tendency to be 'overcome with emotion' would be nonproductive in an environment of noncertainty and occasional serious deprivation, particularly during the very cold winters of the area. Some of this same kind of emotional control seems to be characteristic of people who live on the land in a harsh climate and survive its exigencies.

Competition

In mainstream culture competition is promoted, regarded as desirable, and those who compete successfullly are rewarded. The competitive drive stands behind some of our institutionalization of failure. If some are to win some must lose. The traditional Menominee do not look at matters this way. There is no point in competing with other people because one who competes and 'wins' will be brought down by sorcery. This makes possible some degree of cooperation despite the strong autonomy of the individual person. Like most other attributes it has an adaptive function in the particular circumstances of the group.

Control of Nature

The traditional Menominee would rather walk through a forest than cut it down. They have taken what nature provides in unchanged form and adapted it to their needs. Their economy is not exploitive or transformative. Since all life is considered sacred, one gives when one takes. If one kills a deer, one makes a tobacco sacrifice and utters a prayer to the master of the game of which the deer is a part. Nature can be manipulated to some extent by proper rituals and states of mind, but this control is really a reinforcement of processes already under way. There is not the massive and often very destructive intervention that characterizes the mainstream use of nature.

The Future

The traditional Menominee live in the present whereas mainstream America lives in the future. Even though our anticipation of the future may not always be optimistic we are planning for the future most of our waking hours. Most of our anxieties are about something that hasn't happened yet. The Menominee take the present as given and the future as unknowable. In fact, for most Native American cultures the future is a continuing extension of the present just as it is of the past. The sharp divisions characteristic of Western cultures between past, present and future are not a part of their cosmology. In work with the Menominee, the Blood Indians of Alberta, Canada, and the Mistassini Cree of Quebec this difference in time orientation seemed very important. With the Blood it was not possible to talk about a conditional future. We were engaged one summer in an economic development program. We wanted to find out what the Blood, including the traditional Blood, would do if certain conditions were altered and certain opportunities provided. We became acutely aware of the fact that questioning along these lines with the traditional Blood was futile. They accepted what was in the present and would make no conditional claims upon the future.

Religious Beliefs

It may seem strange to include 'simple religious beliefs' among the American mainstream characteristics. It is not that Christianity is simple or that Western or mainstream American theology is simple. We are referring here to the religious beliefs of the individuals. Most mainstream Americans have a simple faith, an ambivalent faith, or no faith at all. Many have a very generalized concept of God but are not too sure how to approach him (or her). The Menominee, as individuals, participate in a very complex organization of ideas about the supernatural. Their concept of the universe is stratified and humans occupy just one of the seven strata. There are a multitude of spirits and 'deities' with different roles — some good and some evil. The universe itself is saturated with power that humans can dip into by rituals and humility. The understandings are so complex that most people under fifty do not claim to know enough to talk about them. They referred us to the 'old people'. Only old men and old women know enough to speak with authority. It is also dangerous to claim knowledge that one does not fully control. The average traditional Menominee 'citizen' knows much more of their total religious belief system than most mainstream Americans know about theirs.

Technology

The same kind of thing can be said about technology. Americans have a very complex technology, but most of us do not know much about it. We peer under the hood of the car when something goes wrong and despair at the complex labyrinth of hoses and wires and protruding pieces of metal confronting us. The technology is so complex that it is beyond most mainstream Americans. In traditional Menominee culture, the technology was just complicated enough to work well in the environment, and every person knew how to manage it. The Menominee were and are hunters and fishers and gatherers. The tools they use today such as shotguns and fishing lines, are taken over from mainstream technology. But old ways survive in snares that are set upon game trails, yokes for carrying pails of water, fish weirs, and styles of hunting.

Sexual Repression

According to our chart sexual repression is evident on both sides. Briefly, the mainstream does not appear to be in a period of deep sexual repression at present, but the explosion of sexuality may be a response to repression. Also, the repression and displacement of full mature sexuality seems to be operating behind a facade of libertarian behaviors. The age of prudery is not far behind us. Bikinis are small not only because they are more comfortable (more frequently they are not) but because they are a kind of confrontation with our past. Furthermore, we may see a resurgence of sexual repression as the threats of social diseases and particularly the Human Immunodeficiency Virus (HIV) becomes understood better by everyone.

The traditional Menominee were sexually repressed in the sense that they were prudish about full nudity and even about contact during sexual intercourse. During courtship, young men carried a flute to serenade the object of their affections and brought a blanket with them — a finely tanned doe skin with a hole in the center through which the penis could be inserted during intercourse. When a baby boy was born the grandmother would pinch his penis and say 'Don't grow too big and don't lead this little boy astray'. Girls were 'preached to', when they approached their first menstruation, about relations with the opposite sex, their habits, and the dangers of unregulated love making. As one informant said, 'We were taught not to act like dogs but to think about what we were doing'.

Resolutions

The confrontation of cultures that we have described is so profound that it is almost correct to say that there is no way to be a good Menominee in the traditional sense and a good mainstream American simultaneously. The hazards of adaptation that have been created by these sharp and dramatic differences are great. Not all Native American cultures were inimical to mainstream culture. Among the Blood Indians, for example, aggression is expressed, and they are very expressive. Further, their concept of individualism was much closer to mainstream concepts than Menominee autonomy. Though there were important differences and conflicts, it seemed much more likely that a Blood would make an adaptation to the mainstream that could be productive. In fact our study shows that such productive adaptations occurred frequently.

We have said that the Menominee/mainstream cultural confrontation is more extreme than the profile of conflicts characterizing other minorities in their relationships with the mainstream. However, there is in all cases some expression of similar phenomena. Cultural differences do not explain all aspects of minority/mainstream relations, for there are always economic and political factors that enter into the interaction. Nevertheless the cultural process is always present, and we are orienting our model and our explanations around it.

In the Menominee situation and the other two Native American populations in which we have done intensive work we have noted certain types of adaptation to confrontation and conflict. These same types of adaptation are represented in various forms among all minorities in their relationships with the mainstream.

These adaptations or 'adaptive strategies', as we came to think of them, are the following: reaffirmation; selective synthesis; segmentalization; anomic withdrawal; biculturalism; constructive marginality; and compensatory adoption.

Reaffirmation

The reaffirmative adaptation is represented by the 'native-oriented' group. As we have said, there were a few older people in this group who were essentially cultural 'survivors' from the traditional past. There were a larger number of younger people who had met mainstream culture head-on in schools and in the work world and who were trying to recreate and sustain a recognizable Menominee way of life — and escape from the mainstream. They sought participation in the Dream Dance, Medicine Lodge, Chief's Dance, Ghost Feast and tried to live 'Indian style'. They were fully aware of their choice, which we called a 'strategy' of adaptation because of their awareness.

There is something quite similar to this strategy of reaffirmation among non-Indian minorities in any instance where there is a reaffirmation of traditional cultural behaviors or symbols. Within this broad framework, all moves towards the reassertion of ethnic identity would be forms of reaffirmative adaptation. When carried to extremes it represents a deep rejection of adaptation to the mainstream. Such extremes would be represented by the Hutterites and the Amish and, in a different way, by many of the communes of young people that sprang up around the countryside in the 1960s. This rejection is also expressed by the Black Muslims, by the proliferation of fundamentalist sects and even by TV evangelism. In all of these instances there is an attempt to reaffirm some identity that is believed to have once existed and that is divergent from, in some contrast to, and in some degree of confrontation with current mainstream expectations and values.

In an interesting reversal of this relationship, the mainstream is rejecting minority and ethnic cultural attributes and reaffirming traditional values and symbols. The recent diatribes about cultural literacy and the emotionalized concerns expressed about pollution of the required university level Western culture programs by the inclusion of contributions of 'ethnics' or women constitute a rejection of the increasing cultural diversity of America. The then Education Secretary William Bennett spoke at Stanford University on April 18, 1988, against the recent reform of the freshman 'Western Culture' curriculum at Stanford, comparing the reforms to Vichy France, and called the reform an 'assault on western culture' made out of 'ignorance, irrationality, and intimidation'. His attack on the Stanford reforms was broadcast on television by Robert MacNeil the next night (April 19). This media event was followed, as indeed it had been preceded, by wide-ranging comments in the press, many of them critical of Stanford's curricular reform. Stanford President Donald Kennedy's response, a careful defense of the reform, was also cited, but the real attention-getter was Secretary Bennett's remarks, cast in a context already prepared by Alan Bloom's *The Closing of the American Mind* and a plethora of other writings on 'cultural literacy' and the academic decline of the west. An effective reply is made by a collection of minority scholars in *Multicultural Literacy: Opening the American Mind* (Simonson and Walker).

Synthesis

The synthesizing adaptation is not as easy to identify. Among the Menominee it is represented by the Peyote Cult or Native American Church. Menominee Peyotism synthesizes Christian and traditional Menominee belief and symbolism. The Peyote teepee, for example, has thirteen poles, one for Christ and twelve for the disciples. God and Christ are prayed to but the search for power is traditional Menominee. Peyotism is also a kind of revitalization, but purposefully accepts ideological and ritual aspects of mainstream culture. TV evangelism does something like this by combining the Christian gospel and rock-music styles, symbols of material success, and Bible-based orthodoxy.

Withdrawal

Various forms of withdrawal are to be seen among the Menominee people that we have characterized as transitional — meaning transitional from a traditional culture to a mainstream-oriented one. Many of these poeple were so torn by conflict that they could not identify with either the traditional or mainstream cutural symbols or groups. Some drank to oblivion and sometimes death. Others did nothing but vegetate. There are individuals of this kind in any minority group. Their adaptive strategies are self-destructive because the conflict is too much to handle and the opportunities for self development are blocked. The mounting problems of drug abuse and alcoholism, not only among minorities, but among mainstream communities may be considered to be in part due to a loss of cultural guidelines and commitments. Culture provides not only goals, but the instrumental avenues to their achievement. If these avenues are badly damaged, absent, or blocked, the reaction may be to withdraw from the arena of conflict.

Biculturalism

Biculturalism is a viable adaptation for some individuals. Among the Menominee and all of the other Native American groups that we have observed or worked with there were a number of bicultural individuals who were quite at home in either the traditional or mainstream mode. These remarkable people could be called '200 per cent-ers' because they controlled two cultures; they knew when and how to code switch from one context to another. One day at a Medicine Lodge meeting, for example, we saw a well-dressed man drive up in a Cadillac, go into a nearby house, and come out dressed in moccasins and other clothing appropriate to participation in the lodge, which he then entered. It turned out that he was a Milwaukee executive who had maintained close ties with traditional elements of his cultural group. When he came into the Medicine Lodge he was a 100 per cent traditional Potawatomi. (The Potawatomi joined together with the Menominee and other Central Algonkians for such ceremonies.) Of thirteen adult Menominee males in the most acculturated category of persons, with whom we worked intensively, four of them were bicultural in this manner. Of course, individuals may be only partially bicultural and present a much more segmentalized adaptation, with bits and pieces of culture from both frames of reference, but without the ability to make a complete switch from one to the other.

Biculturalism as an adaptive mode has been noted by many observers of minority adaptations. Though it can produce good results, it is an additional strain on the individual who has to master two cultural codes. If these two codes are as different from each other as most Native American codes are from the mainstream ones, this is difficult. For people like some Rumanians and Hungarians, who were born and raised in border areas where code switching through several more or less related cultural codes is the rule, the problem is not so difficult. For others, however, the added stress can be quite significant.

Constructuve Marginality

Constructive marginality is represented by a number of Menominee who made a viable adaptation to culture conflict by avoiding strong identification with any group or any one set of symbols. They can form a personal culture that is instrumentally productive but that is usually constituted of several different segments, some of them mainstream. They distance themselves in greater and lesser degrees from much of the conflict and maintain a wry and perhaps cynical view of it. Constructive marginality may be a useful adaptive strategy for some minorities, or for anyone in conflict with the value orientations and pivotal dialogue of the mainstream. It is likely, however, to result in a lowering of commitment to any particular goals and to the personal and social action related to them.

Compensatory Adaptation

The compensatory adaptation mode or strategy was observed among the most highly acculturated Menominee. Among them there were some '150 per cent-ers' — people who were more respectable than most respectable mainstream Whites and who wondered how we could live and work with 'those dirty Indians'. They were *compensators*.

There were others who were undifferentiated culturally from mainstream Whites in the surrounding area and who did not denigrate others who were more traditional. In fact they were interested in Menominee traditions, as described by anthropologists such as Walter Hoffman, Alanson Buck Skinner, and Felix Keesing.

The difference between these two kinds of highly acculturated persons was that the compensators appeared to be individuals who had suffered at some time in their lives because of their identification as Indians, particularly in early school experience. They spent considerable amounts of their energy convincing themselves and others that they were just as good as anyone else.

The counselor of the eighth grade children described in the previous chapter was just such an individual. She was an Italian-American, not a Native American, but the dynamics of compensation are the same.

One of the problems that can be encountered in the use of native teachers from anywhere in the world is that they may be compensators and be unintentionally prejudiced toward children exhibiting traditional or 'ethnic' cultural patterns in their behavior. Compensators may appear in various guises and from various origins; some workaholics are compensators as are some politicians. Compensation is a personal psychological adaptation that is frequently, though not always, the product of cultural conflict, particularly the experience of personal denigration resulting from such conflict.

On the other hand, those individuals among the Menominee who were highly acculturated and *not* compensators were people who had been raised by parents who had already attained considerable instrumental command of the mainstream culture and who were able to pass this command over to their children without loading it with compensatory feeling states.

Interpretation

A personally viable adaptation may occur in any of these categories, excepting possibly that of withdrawal. And even here it is conceivable that an individual can withdraw without this withdrawal being self-destructive. The hermit is a classic form of this adaptation. All social and emotional adaptations are a function of the need of individuals to retain self-esteem. The quest for self-esteem is a basic motive in both achievement and self-destruction. It is even possible to regard suicide as a last, desperate, attempt to salvage self-esteem. The excessive use of alcohol and drugs is often related to a need to heighten, at least temporarily, a sense of self-esteem. This heightened sense soon degrades into self-recrimination but, lacking other developed avenues to the attainment of self-esteem, drugs and alcohol can help for a little while. A reaffirmative adaptation is clearly an attempt to salvage self-esteem by withdrawing from and excluding the alien culture, thereby resolving the conflict by reidentifying with traditional elements.

As we observe alienation and the number of drop-outs in our schools we are inclined to think that the relationships we have described between Menominee culture as a type case and mainstream culture are not dissimilar to those experienced by children in the school. We do not wish to argue for a single factor model of analysis. There are many factors involved in alienation and dropping out. However, as we review the scene, we see cultural divergences, conflicts, and confrontations as a part of the interaction that results in a variety of these adaptive strategies being utilized. A child who drops out of school may be showing himself, his friends and the teachers that he has an identity, a self, that the school has not recognized. Blacks, Chicanos, and American Indians have told us that the reason they dropped out of school was because their peers thought they were 'selling out' by staying in school and trying to do well. Conversely, some have told us that they stayed in school and did succeed academically but in the process lost contact with their peers, friends, and even families.

The much-vaunted success of some of the new immigrant minorities such as the Vietnamese and Punjabis seems to be due to the fact that success in school does not mean alienation from friends and family but quite the opposite. Success in school is an achievement that is supported by and contributes to the family's sense of definition and pride.

Notes

See G. and L. Spindler (1984) for a description of the 'native-oriented', and the other groups in the Menominee community. An application of the adaptive types we found among the Menominee to the analyses of the adaptations by ethnic minorities in the schools is made in G. and L. Spindler (1987c). Some comparisons of Menominee and Blood (Kanai) Indian adaptations are drawn in G. and L. Spindler (1978). The contributions of Walter Hoffman, Alanson Buck Skinner, and Felix Keesing, early observers of the Menominee, are cited in G. Spindler (1955). The relative success of Vietnamese, Punjabis, and other recent immigrants to the U.S. is discussed by Margaret Gibson and John Ogbu in Jacob and Jordan (1987).

Chapter 7

Religious Movements in America

Introduction

To analyze religious movements in America is indeed a large order. The United States has been the site of many movements, many of them fundamentalist in character and some of them imported from cultures quite alien to Euro-American concepts.

We will touch upon three kinds of religious movements that seem to represent important variants characterizing the American religious scene. Those movements are the Hare Krsna religious cult; the Holy Ghost, or Snake Handlers cult; and current television evangelism (televangelism).

No attempt will be made to deal with the established traditional religious institutions in the United States, though they are undeniably an important part of our culture. Much of the so called 'work ethic' or 'protestant work ethic' for example, stems historically from Calvinism, and is considered to have been essential to the development of modern capitalism.

The established Protestant and Catholic churches have historically been at the center of American communities, though their influence has weakened over the past few decades. Nevertheless, in most small and middle-sized American communities today, the churches are still pivotal centers in the maintenance of respectable cultural values and behaviors.

The recent explosion of interest and participation in TV worship, with its dramatic evangelical thrust, has eroded the influence of the more staid churches. At the same time it shows us that interest in religion has not faded in America. In times of stress religion becomes particularly important but the highly institutionalized forms seem less effective than the more personal and dynamic ones.

Hare Krsna Cult

The Hare Krsna cult (The International Society for Krsna Consciousness) began in the United States in 1965 when it was brought from India by His Divine Grace A.C. Bhaktivedanta Swami Prabhupada. Since then it has proliferated, though it has probably passed the zenith of its prominence. One encounters the cult's devotees in airports and other public places, selling pamphlets and books in order to raise funds. The saffron robed young people on the streets of some American cities, chanting and supplicating for money, are a familiar sight. The cult, with its emphasis upon religious forms and symbols quite alien to staid Protestantism or respectable Catholicism, seems very foreign and perhaps even threatening. The young people who enter the cult shave their heads, don foreign garb, chant incessantly, and seem to have left their relatives, friends, and families permanently.

Devotion to Hare Krsna requires an immersion of the self, a giving up of individuality, and unceasing ritualized, religious practice that allows little time for personal reflection. As in many of the cults that have appeared on the American scene over the past few years, the activity of the devoted participant seems designed to blot out competing thoughts or distracting notions.

Sexual activity and sexuality among the 'Children of Krsna' (the title of a case study by Francine Daner) are underplayed, which seems strange given the pronounced eroticism of many Hindu religious symbols and forms. Family relationships are discouraged and children seem to be more or less irrelevant. The position of women is not particularly exalted either. Though some other religious developments have stressed sexual equality, it does not seem apparent among the children of Krsna. Women are often assigned the more menial duties and are regarded as serving a 'higher principle' when they perform these duties.

With these patterns dominating the behavior and symbolism of the Hare Krsna cult, one might conclude that it is decidedly non-American. As in many ritual and ideological forms that appear within larger social frameworks, appearances do not tell the whole story. In the emphasis upon piety, devotion, selflessness, poverty of the individual, ritualized hard work, and even in the emphasis on the male rather than the female principle, the Hari Krsna cult may appear as a disguised reaffirmative movement. Since most of the devotees originate from middle class, even upper-middle class mainstream families, and are of almost exclusively North European Anglo-Saxon Protestant in origin, this is not surprising.

In some respects the Hare Krsna cult appears to be a special version of 'hippie-ism'. Hippies virtually became extinct in the US during the 1980s, but during the 1960s and 1970s they seemed to be everywhere. There was no strict code as for the Hare Krsna, and no universal ritual forms. Nevertheless, in hippie communes there were rituals usually involving the sacrament of 'grass', or marijuana. The long discussion, or 'rap' session held over most evenings, was predictable and, in some communes, almost as sacred as a religious ritual. Furthermore, hippie communes stressed aestheticism, pietism of a sort, the immolation of the individual (in certain ways) in the community, a search for self knowledge, the sharing of goods and services (including sexual services), and a generalized anti-intellectual orientation.

Both Hare Krsna and hippie-ism may be considered counter-cultural movements. The implicatons of 'counter-cultural' are not, however, entirely correct. The outward forms of respectable, middle class, mainstream culture were indeed 'countered' but they were transmuted into other forms within the actual practice within these movements. Both may, in a sense, be considered reaffirmative movements because certain aspects of their symbolism, ideology, and behavior reaffirmed the earlier pietism of religious fundamentalism in America.

America has a fundamentalist inheritance, a pattern of orthodoxy and literality, anti-intellectualism, and rejection of competing ideas, starting with the early Puritans, and continuing to the present. Many people who came to America as immigrants throughout the sixteenth, seventeenth, eighteenth and early nineteenth centuries came because of religious persecution. They were being persecuted for beliefs and practices that countered the institutionalized church ideologies and doctrines of the period in Europe and England. American fundamentalism also seems to be nourished by the ambiguities and uncertainties of the American scene. It provides certainty and 'answers' in the midst of uncertainty.

The Holy Ghost Cult

When one sees the members of the cult variously named the Church of God, the Snake Handling cult, or the Holy Ghost Church, dancing in a trance state, handling rattlesnakes of all sizes, and drinking strychnine in the film *Holy Ghost People*, it is hard to believe that they represent a religious movement with deep roots in American culture.

The Church of God is a specialized version of the Pentecostal groups that subscribe to the belief that the Holy Spirit actually descended on the Apostles. Pentecostal groups in turn, were unique outshoots of Methodism. They were reformed groups with focus on individual experience, as is characteristic of most fundamentalist movements of Protestant origin. Methodism was originally brought to South Carolina from England in 1777 by John Wesley. He was later asked to leave because of improper conduct with the ladies among his followers. The movement, however, remained.

The rural South where the Church of God/Snake-Handling cult originated was a stonghold of the low church sects such as the Southern Baptist and Methodist. The Holy Ghost people are also a branch of another fundamentalist movement — the Holy Roller Church. Like others, the 'Holy Rollers' hold revivalistic meetings where faith healings occur and where there are explicit sermons against dancing, drinking, smoking, and even movies. But in the cult context, it is possible to have ecstatic experiences, to have seizures, go into trance, and be possessed by the Holy Spirit. It is possible to 'speak in tongues' — to use glossolalia, — a rapid monotonous chant with a special cadence and rhythm using, as perceived by non-believers, certain meaningless nonsense syllables repetitively. The performance of gifted glossolalic speakers is impressive to watch and to hear. The do indeed seem possessed. When there was an outbreak of it in the high Episcopal Church some years ago, Bishop Pike mounted a special investigation.

The Holy Ghost people are like the Holy Rollers in most respects but are unique to fundamentalist movements due to the introduction of snake handling, the swallowing of poison, and the use of fire to test one's faith. The cult was founded in 1909 by George Hensley in Grasshopper Valley, Tennessee. One hot summer day a text from the Bible kept coming back to him from Mark XVI: 17–18.

> In my name shall they cast out devils. They shall speak with new tongues. They shall take up serpents and if they drink any deadly thing it shall not hurt them.

Mr. Hensley found a large rattlesnake and began his evangelical work, thrusting it at potential converts and fondling it himself. The Snake Handling cult spread. After ten years it was temporarily suspended because a participant was bitten and died. The fatalities from being bitten by these venomous snakes have ranged over the entire history of the cult; reconstructing their incidence, about three out of one hundred believers are bitten. It is difficult to understand why the snakes do not bite their handlers more often. As shown in the film, *The Holy Ghost People*, there seems no reason why everyone should not be bitten repeatedly. Snakes are handled in every conceivable way, even thrown about from one participant to another. But at the end of the film when a 'leader' who is not exactly a preacher, a kindly, guitar-carrying man, is standing before his congregation, when there is no music, no dancing and no movement, he is bitten. His arm and hand swell during the few minutes left to the filming. He did not die, but he looked 'mighty sick'.

Mr. Hensley died in 1955, and later so did his son, both from snake bites. Since the cult is outlawed in most states it has gone underground but despite, or perhaps because of, this suppression the membership appears to have increased.

With the hazards to one's health involved in cult participation, why do people continue to join and practice these behaviors? It is characteristic of all religious belief systems that negative evidence can be explained away or interpreted as support for beliefs and dogma. In fact, all organized ideologies, whether religious, political, or personal seem to have this quality. When someone is bitten by one of the snakes being handled, it is a test, and if the faith of the person bitten is strong enough he or she survives. It is evidence of God's will and not something that ordinary mortals can question. If the victim dies it is also God's will and not to be questioned.

Leon Festinger's early study, *When Prophecy Fails*, demonstrated that even the failure of the predictions by the prophets that the world would end on a certain day at a certain time increased the membership of this cult. Each time the latest prophecy failed the membership increased. It seems to be human nature that when people are devoted to a belief, a cause, or even to another person, negative evidence is swept away again and again and frequently only deepens the commitment.

This brings us to the question of recruitment. Why do people join fundamentalist movements, or for that matter, any social or political or religious movement? Weston LaBarre, the author of the book *They Shall Take Up Serpents*, opts for a psycho-social explanation. He interprets the behaviors of the members and of the minister as involving considerable sublimated sex. Neither the minister nor the members are conscious of this and would deny it if it was brought to their attention. LaBarre develops a good case for psycho-social recruitment, with case studies of individuals and observations of their behavior. This type of explanation involves the notion that recruitment depends upon pathology. A certain number of individuals with pathological sexual adjustment are attracted to the cult and commit themselves to it as a defense against their pathology. The cult permits them to express this pathology, but in unrecognized forms.

Within this framework even the handling of snakes may be considered to be sexual in character. The snake is a symbol of the phallus. Phallic symbolism is common throughout the world and frequently in religious cults. Ancient practices such as circumcision may be interpreted as symbolically equivalent to the shedding of the snake's skin. Scepters may be seen as disguised phalluses evoking images of strength and potency. Church steeples may even be thought of as phallic. For most people, this is probably going too far, but the potential power of such explanations should not be denied. Symbolism involving all sorts of motives and their transformation make social and religious behavior predictable, controllable, and interesting.

Another explanation probably more favored by most social scientists is that of 'relative deprivation'. The members of the Holy Ghost cult are very poor. They originate from sections of the rural South and particularly Appalachia where the soil is depleted, the forests have been cut, mining is dying, and there is virtually no industry. They see themselves as not only poor, but as poor in comparison to others towards whom they feel superior, particularly Blacks and Native Americans. People who experience relative deprivation may engage in compensatory adaptations such as the Snake Handling cult. It is something that they have that not everybody else does. And the excitement of dancing, singing, and ecstatic seizures make up somewhat for the drabness and poverty of their lives.

Further, and importantly, the cult gives its members hope. There is a better world, there is a way to reach it, there are beliefs that seem true, and there is faith to sustain one through self doubt, anxiety, and loss of self-esteem. There is also the security of affiliation with others. When the members of this cult enter their church the men kiss each other full on the mouth, an act unlikely to occur outside the confines of the cult, especially in the culture from which its members are drawn. There are constant expressions of interdependence and friendship. Collections are taken to ease the economic burden for members who had to travel a long distance or who have suffered particularly severe economic reverses. Furthermore, there is no lordly priest with the trappings of authority but rather each individual has direct access to wisdom, salvation, and sacred power through the Holy Ghost.

Particularly impressive to us, as anthropologists who have studied religious activity in other cultures, is the fact that so much of what the Holy Ghost people and Pentecostalists in general do, say, and believe, is similar to the religious movements in other changing cultures. The Peyote cult or Native American church, among the Menominee Indians, is a good example.

The Peyote cult and the Holy Ghost cult are very different in symbolism, and in specific ritual content and beliefs. The Menominee Peyotists meet in a Plains Indian teepee, partake of the Peyote cactus bud as a sacrament and have Peyote-induced visions but do not handle snakes, and are quiet and prayerful. The Holy Ghost people are ecstatic and sing, play guitars, dance, and go into trances. Despite these differences, there is an underlying similarity. The similarity is in the fact that both groups approach salvation and insight on an individual basis. Though the Holy Ghost people accept some portions of the Bible in their literal phrasing, there is great latitude in how, when, and with what results one will approach the blessings of salvation and even possession by the Holy Spirit. The Peyotists sometimes use the Bible in ritual, but usually only as a symbol. No one reads from it or tries to interpret it. One takes peyote and sometimes has hallucinations, since the peyote bud is a hallucinogen, and searches for power in the American Indian manner. For the Holy Ghost people, the search is for salvation, as it is frequently for the Menominee Peyotists, and the salvation itself allows for participation in power through possession by the Holy Spirit.

Both the members of the Holy Ghost Church and the Menominee Peyotists are poor in the mainstream, material sense. They both see around them other populations that are not intrinsically different but who are much better off. For the Menominee, Peyotism may be a compensation for loss. As many Peyotists have told us, 'You White people have everything else. You have the land, the forest, the animals of the forest, the waters, and the fish of the waters, but we have our own religion.' Both sects have sought for and attained a unique status, a special blessing, that is not shared with the very people with whom they are contrasting themselves. Both sects furnish the individual with a strong sense of affiliation. A believer has friends who are closer, even, than relatives, and he or she can acknowledge weakness, sorrow, disappointment and receive recognition, praise, and blessings through participation in their faith.

Perhaps the basic urge underlying all religious participation is to reduce anxiety about the unknown and the unknowable, to find surcease from the trials and tribulations of everyday life, to assuage disappointment and hurt, to receive recognition both from one's fellows and from God or the equivalent. Churches were discouraged in post-Revolutionary Soviet Russia because they were considered to be 'placebos' for the masses. People sought in religious experience solutions to problems that could better be sought in economic and political reform. Whether we agree with the early Soviets or not, it seems quite correct that religious participation and devotion can make up for a lot of deficits in the outside world of everyday life.

The important points to carry along with us are that even such extreme forms as the Hare Krsna and the Holy Ghost cult are not in themselves such radical departures from a fundamentalist orientation that has always been a part of American religious action and ideology. The extreme forms such as these seem to be produced under conditions of stress and threat. They do not, however, constitute a sharp break with the past. There is psychocultural continuity. The other important point is that the specific content, and the specific forms of ideology may be uniquely American, but at the same time they may be seen as universal phenomena answering human needs that are produced by social, economic, political, forces over which one has little or no control.

Televangelism

It seems a far cry from Holy Ghost and Peyote cults to the glossy, professional performances of the televangelists in their TV-stage 'churches'. One hears the overtones of gospel singing that are not too far removed from the singing of the Black Southern Baptists. The accompanying music is also derivative; although it is similar to popular mainstream rock'n'roll, it is softened and made palatable for the evangelist's audience. One hears the exhortations of persuasive men and women who talk of their feelings, give anecdotes from their own experience, or make up new ones as needed, describe conversion and salvation, urge their viewers to give, give, give, the better to receive.

Televangelism is closer to the Holy Ghost cult than it is to the Menominee Peyote cult. The latter is too solemn, too prayerful, too individualistic. In the Peyote cult participating members spend a great deal of their time bowed over, with their foreheads nearly touching the ground and praying in barely audible tones to their gods in their own language and their own way. The televangelists, in contrast, wave their arms, shout, and sing in unison. They also give together and receive.

In one night of televison watching, we saw one prominent TV church gather pledges of nearly 2,000,000 dollars. These pledges were not from rich people who could give without hurting. Perhaps they were people who followed the speaker's advice and stopped using their credit cards and paying interest. He urged them to use the money thus saved to make contributions to his church. Televangelism in America reached gigantic fiscal proportions during its heyday. Millions of people watched, participated vicariously, sent in contributions, or came to the 'citadels' themselves and made contributions.

They give and what do they receive? Like the Peyotists and the Holy Ghost cult participants they receive a sense of affiliation. They are not alone. They can receive blessings by concentrated effort and participation, and by believing. There is a strong fundamentalist ethos in televangelism. Though there is a lot of room for personal anecdotes, individualistic performances, idiosyncratic rituals, there is an underlying reference to and persistent belief in a literal interpretation of at least selected passages from the Holy Bible.

Seen in this way televangelism is, like the Peyote cult of the Menominee, a kind of synthesis. It is composed of configurations from several potentially opposing forces. Fundamentalism, in its original pietistic forms in America, as with the Puritans, was duller, repressed, harsh, and withdrawn from sensual pleasures. The Black Baptist Church, in contrast, is often equally fundamentalist, but is expressive, exhibitionistic, joyous, ecstatic. The Holy Ghost sect tends more towards the latter than the former. Televangelism combines the best of two worlds. It is joyous, it is colorful, it satisfies the senses, it provides entertainment and excitement, and it demands orthodoxy of belief. Fundamentalism in America has found a new and effective form and it appeals to the American imagination and need.

It provides its followers with excitement, affiliation, salvation, and a kind of power. Televangelism can make up for the pervasive sense of loss, of insecurity, of generalized anxiety, that is a part of the daily life of most persons in today's America. Televangelism also provides images of success and achievement. The palatial and colorful TV stages are no mean and paltry shacks inhabited by the poor. They represent and demonstrate material success. They are a special representation of the 'American dream'.

Televangelism is like the Holy Ghost sect and in a very different way like the Menominee Peyote cult. The values represented in the Holy Ghost meetings are those of the mainstream. Individualism, independence, resistance to authority, the desirability of success, are all portrayed and exhibited in manifold ways. If one listens to the personal testimonies of members, as in the film we have referred to previously, *The Holy Ghost People*, we can hear these values resonating. For the Menominee the values and behaviors are different, and appropriate to the Menominee heritage, even though they are combined with Christian heritage, but the symbolism and ritual as well as the professed ideology all resonate with traditional Menominee Indian values and assumptions. Televangelism does this in modern terms but combines entertainment and fiscal success with a fundamentalist orthodoxy of professed belief. This is a remarkable accomplishment and seems to account for the success of televangelism, particularly in parts of the country where life is particularly uncertain but the glittering goals of material success are more than abundant — such as the West coast, particularly Southern California, and parts of Texas.

Televangelism is not now (1990) what it was only a year or two ago. The fall of some of its most famous promoters occasioned by personal scandals and questions about fiscal matters has tarnished its image. Thousands have turned away from it but thousands remain faithful. The need for the reassurance of orthodoxy and the search for affiliation are there. Another movement will be cast up by our dynamic culture.

Psychological and Value Interactions

Fundamentalism in its modern form, but as a constant American religious orientation, is comprised of two groups who share a counterculture, but each of whom has its own social dynamic. The lower class sect-type churches, such as the Holy Ghost Church, compensate for and adapt to socioeconomic deprivation. These churches provide social cohesion and support and a social outlet for repressed emotions. It is significant that the theologies of these sects tend to promote the values of the culture at large and are a socializing medium for converting lower class values to dominant middle class values.

In contrast, the mainline fundamentalists, predominantly white middle-class Americans, suffer from a form of cultural deprivation. The fundamentalist Protestant ethic fit the expanding agrarian frontier and the growth of a capitalist economy emphasizing orderliness, morality, sexual control, individualism, and egalitarianism. As the frontier began to disappear, this system became less relevant and people holding to the old line Protestant ethic found themselves on the fringes of society. In an attempt to reduce cultural dissonance various forms of anti-intellectualism have developed. Conflicting ideas are considered dangerous. The disparity between fundamentalist values and dominant middle class values produces major social or psychological dissonance in the lives of fundamentalists. Orthodoxy, under these conditions, has seemed to be an answer.

Clinical data (Pattison, 1974) indicates that the children of fundamentalist parents who are defined as a religious minority have experienced low self-esteem, high anxiety, psychosomatic symptoms, and depression. They have an impersonal relationship between reward and punishment. The children are led to believe that only God can reward or punish. They see the outside world as comprised of hostile, attacking people while they are taught to repress hostility and aggression. It is these kinds of repressions that lead to psychosomatic ailments.

The interpretation above is drawn from psychiatric analytic sources and would probably be rejected by many social scientists who favor socioculturally oriented analyses. However, it is included here to demonstrate possible relationships between personal adaptation and religious participation and conviction. The two can never be entirely separated.

We are also concerned with the relationship between value systems and the personal experience of fundamentalism, including evangelistic forms. Most participants and followers of televangelism appear to be persons imbued with middle-class American values, therefore mainstream values, but particularly in their lower-middle class forms.

The lower-middle class in America has historically suffered from anxiety about class and socio-economic position. Every economic downturn threatens to unseat them and every economic upturn makes them feel that they have not succeeded quite enough. They teeter on the brink of lower class status and aspire to higher class status. When times become uncertain they will be the social class and socioeconomic status most threatened and they will turn, according to this analysis, to religion. But they will not turn to the conventional, orthodox, staid, institutionalized, religious forms. They will turn to religious forms that promise success in its most exhibitionist and dramatic form. Televangelists themselves are the epitome of success. They are rich and flaunt it, they command great resources, and they demonstrate their commitment to millions of viewers each week. They also fall hard when they fall.

By sending their money in to a television evangelist and his or her church, these people can also participate in success. At the same time, they receive a sense of belonging to something bigger and more powerful than themselves. It is no wonder that people look for and find comfort in this particular form of vital, dramatic, orthodoxy.

Conclusion

We have not pretended to provide an adequate analysis of all religions in contemporary America. This is not only more than this small book could contain but it is beyond our competence as anthropologists. What we have tried to do is to select a few important dimensions of contemporary movements in America and relate them to base social and economic conditions as well as attend, in some degree, to the psychological processing of such phenomenon by individuals. Our analysis may be contested from a number of different points of view including those of the participants in religious forms of these kinds themselves. Nevertheless these are some of the considerations that, we feel, need to be considered in a holistic analysis of such phenomenon.

Notes

The Hare Krsna cult is described by Francine Daner (1976). Hippie culture in one prominent (Gainsville, Florida) community is described by William Partridge (1973). The Holy Ghost, Church of God, including John Wesley's part in its history, is analyzed by Weston LaBarre. His analysis is more psychoanalytic than ours. Leon Festinger (1956) treats with the social psychology of prophecy. The film by Peter Adair (1976) provides an intimate and moving look at a meeting where there are trance states, rattlesnake handling, guitar music and 'White gospel' singing. Chapter 3, 'The Peyote Road', in *Dreams with Power*, G. and L. Spindler (1984) interprets the Menominee peyote cult. The clinical data on the children of fundamentalist parents is discussed by Pattison (1974).

Chapter 8

The American Hinterland

Roseville and Environs

Roseville, a village in Wisconsin, is approached on the state highway as it curves and climbs through the countryside. There are dairy farms, some with three or four silos attached to the barn (to store cut fodder), some with one silo, and a few with none. The number of silos is an indication of the size of the operation. A three silo farm is likely to have about a hundred head of milking cows and about 300 or more acres of land, most of it used as pasture for corn and for hay. There is usually a woodlot. These are not farms where food is produced in gardens and pigs and chickens are kept to feed the family. They are farms where milk is produced to obtain cash. They are big businesses.

There are many smaller farms, some of them run on a part-time basis by people who work in towns forty miles or more distant. On these farms the family is likely to produce at least garden vegetables and there are frequently chickens and sometimes a few pigs for meat.

Many of the people on these farms work full-time (when they work) but on an intermittent basis in the towns to which they can commute or in the cheese factories. The men often work on construction. Many of them are 'jacks of all trades'. They can do almost anything — fix roofs, pour concrete, do general carpentry, even do wiring — although the building inspector may suggest some changes. They run their smaller farms as they have time and on these farms the woman of the house often does the milking because the man gets back too late from his job.

On one such farm there were only twelve cows being milked, there was no silo, there was a garden about a quarter acre in size and thiry-two chickens. There were a hundred acres of pasture, a corn field, and another eighty acres in wood land, much of it enclosing a small stream that furnished brook trout for the family's table. Usually each hunting season a deer would be taken from the woodlot as well.

The man of the household, Jack, did carpentry and odd jobs nearby when he could. He worked for neighbors when they needed some rough carpentry or a roof repaired. He worked for contractors doing heavy construction in a small city of about 36,000 people, nearly forty-five miles distant. When he worked on such distant construction he would leave by seven o'clock in the morning after milking the twelve cows. He rarely got back before seven o'clock at night and by then his wife, Mary, would have milked them.

Each year Jack and Mary considered giving up the cows, even selling the land, but each year they decided not to do so. We asked them why they kept on. It didn't seem very profitable, but Jack would always say, 'Look at that new car out there. We couldn't have bought that without the milk check. And you saw my new snowmobile? Well that came out of the milk check too.' But when we tried to pin him down about exactly what his cash flow was he was always quite vague.

His land had been inherited from his father, he had no mortgage, his house was fairly old but in good condition (he kept it that way) and he paid no rent. His barn was small and weathered but it had a tight roof and good stalls for the cows and a sound concrete floor and drainage system. He or Mary cleaned the barn every day, taking the manure out in a wheel barrow up a long inclined plane made of planks. When the outside pile got too big, Jack would take it away with his front-end loader (a hydraulic shovel mounted on a tractor) and a manure wagon and distribute it on his alfalfa and corn fields.

Upkeep and overhead were minimal. Though a businessman would regard the farm as a losing proposition because there was no capital being reinvested in the operation, from Jack and Mary's point of view it was their single source of dependable income, not subject to the ups and downs of construction work or neighbors' decisions about building.

There was more to it, however. Jack and Mary had lived on farms all of their lives and they really could not think of themselves as not living on the land and not being farmers. If anyone asked Jack what he did he always said, 'Oh, well, dairy farming.' Although his cash income fom construction work was substantially greater than that derived from his farm, he did not think of himself primarily as a construction worker or even as a carpenter. Of course it is true that Jack's work on construction was intermittent, often amounting to less than six months out of the year. The farm and the cows were always there, requiring attention and producing cash in the form of the milk check.

The state highway forms Roseville's main street where there are two gas stations, one on each side of the road, and two taverns, likewise distributed, a large general store, a recently rebuilt bank, what looks like a used car lot but which is actually a garage, the post office, a small liquor store, and a few small, well kept houses and several quite large ones built probably around the turn of the century.

What is noticeably missing is a medical clinic of any kind — not even a doctor's office or a dentist's office. Also lacking are a public library, a bowling alley or any other large public recreational facility and any form of shopping center other than the general store which mainly sells groceries. There is, however, a good-sized elementary school building with a gymnasium attached to it and a large playing field, one corner of which is laid out in a baseball diamond. There are no tennis courts and no swimming pools but the local mill pond has a removable dock thrust out in it equipped with a diving board. Most of the town's youngsters swim there during the summer.

Roseville is represented by a very competitive baseball team composed of young, and not so young farmers and workers from the area. During the late spring and summer there is almost always a game on the weekend, with supportive wives and families as spectators.

Roseville contains about three hundred houses, virtually all of them in good condition and many of them painted white. The lawns and shrubbery are well kept. The streets are all surfaced with macadam and in some parts of town there are sidewalks. The school itself serves a larger area than Roseville proper — a school district from which it draws about two hundred students distributed throughout eight grades and kindergarten.

Roseville school is staffed by seven teachers, a librarian, a kitchen manager and two helpers and by a number of educational specialists who come in weekly or monthly from the superintendent's office fourteen miles distant, located in the larger town of Arcadia with its approximately 9,000 inhabitants.

Arcadia

In Arcadia, Wisconsin, there is the full range of services available in most American communities. There are shopping centers just outside of the city limits which compete all too successfully with the main street businesses downtown. It is very difficult for the local merchants to meet the prices of the large chain stores that sell everything from groceries to clothing and housewares. They manage somehow to hang on. There are two medical clinics, a general hospital, a number of doctors, several dentists downtown and one dental clinic. If specialty work has to be done that can not be done at the local general hospital, the patient will be sent to nearby Wapeton thiry-five miles away where there are specialists. There are several elementary schools and an aging high school building filled with exuberant young males and females, most of them of Scandinavian, German or Polish extraction.

There are few non-White minorities represented in Arcadia and virtually none in Roseville except for a few Indians. There are a few families that are believed to be 'part Indian' and a few identify themselves as Native Americans. There are no Blacks living in Arcadia and no Mexican Americans. A few appear on the streets as tourists and there are some transient workers, largely Hispanic, who usually stay for only part of the year. The few Indians who live in town are more or less indistinguishable from the rest of the population as far as housing, work habits, and social life are concerned.

There is not a great deal of manufacturing in Arcadia or Roseville, though the latter boasts a sawmill that also produces veneer products. This lumber industry is the mainstay of Roseville's population — that part of it which is not connected directly with agriculture. In Arcadia there are welding work-shops, electrical work-shops, sheetmetal work-shops, garages for the repair of agricultural machinery, a small factory that makes fishing lures, another that manufactures wreathes for funerals, weddings and Christmas, a creamery, and a potato sorting and sacking center. There is a small foundry with heavy metal stamping and working equipment. There are service and sale centers for all of the major types of American cars, and one of them also sells and services foreign ones, but foreign cars are not as popular as on the West and East coasts. There was also a shoe factory and a furniture factory until 1983.

Arcadia is suffering, like most small towns in America are suffering, from a loss of some of its industrial base and a significant decline in agriculture. It is not correct to say that there is less agricultural production. This part of Wisconsin overproduces dairy products. These products are in such surplus that the federal government has to store large quantities of them and try to give them away. But the number of farms and farmers has decreased as some farms have become larger and more business-like and some have failed.

The population of the countryside decreased steadily for years as people left their small farms to go to cities larger than Arcadia for work, but it has increased again lately with an influx of people who buy an acre or two out in the country, build a house, (often starting with a mobile home and then adding on to it) and live there. These people are commuters who may travel fifty or sixty miles to their job. They are people who want to live in the country and whose parents or grandparents did. They say that they want to have space 'for the kids to grow up in'. They regard the hardship of commuting as what they have to pay to live as they want. Most of them have had some experience living and working in Milwaukee or Chicago and regard the city as a kind of hell.

In Arcadia there are poor people and some fairly rich people, if one can judge by their houses and other material possessions. There are young and old people. There are professionals such as doctors, lawyers, dentists and teachers. There are intellectuals who hold a monthly meeting to discuss 'good books'. There are writers, artists, and a very active daily newspaper in the town. There are skilled workers and a few unskilled ones. There are people who are devoutly religious and go to one of the four Protestant churches or two Catholic churches in town, while there are a number of people in both Arcadia and in Roseville and its environs who are members of what the established churches regard as 'off-beat sects'. These people regard themselves as no less respectable and no less 'church-going' than members of the established churches. They are all of Protestant derivation.

There are many more people who do not go to church and do not think about religion very much, but they would be shocked to hear themselves described as atheists or even agnostics. When people die in Roseville or Arcadia or the surrounding countryside, they are buried in a cemetery and with a Christian ritual. Some people never see a minister or a priest until someone in their family dies or gets married. Some of these people make regular contributions to the church even though they don't attend, but others do not. The ministers and priests never deny service to anyone.

In Arcadia there are the usual service organizations such as the Kiwanis and the Elks. There is also the Masonic Lodge and the Knights of Columbus. Most of the business and professional men belong to one of these organizations and their wives belong to their auxiliaries such as the Eastern Star of the Masonic Lodge. Some of the sons of the Masons are already Demolays and will presumably become Masons when they grow up, and their daughters are in the Rainbow Girls, likewise destined for the Eastern Star.

Though the role of these organizations in community life has diminished over the years, (less so for the service organizations than for the quasi-religious ones such as the Masons and the Knights of Columbus) they still play an important role. Many of Arcadia's business and professional affairs are discussed and decisions made within the halls of these organizations. The service organizations are also important contexts for business contacts, discussions, and decision-making.

There is no slum in Arcadia. There are some relatively poor houses in two parts of town but they do not approach the deteriorated conditions of some parts of American inner cities. Most of the homes and properties in Arcadia are very well kept, their lawns landscaped with loving care and sometimes even professional help. Some of the larger homes on Main Street would rival the better homes in a large Mid-western city, but they cost less than half as much.

There is personal security in Arcadia and Roseville and in most of the surrounding countryside. There are few violent crimes, but some robberies. Most people leave their doors unlocked when they make a short trip to their neighbors' homes or to a nearby store, but they would be careful to lock up if they were going away on a trip. No one thinks about getting mugged when one goes out at night and single women stay in their houses without fear. There have been a few instances of extreme violence but usually it was because somebody passed through town who started in Milwaukee and Chicago and was heading 'up North'. There are a few suicides, some violent domestic quarrels, and occasional fights between young bloods at local taverns or at dance halls, but the overall feeling is one of security.

There is not a 'drug problem' but there are drugs. Alcohol is still the most widely abused drug and there are probably as many alcoholics in Arcadia and Roseville as in most places in the country. Most are 'closet alcoholics' however, and alcoholism is not considered to be a community problem. There is some 'grass' smoked by high school students and even in the middle school. Hard drugs such as cocaine and opiates, have made their appearance but they are not widely or consistently abused.

The athletic teams from the high school are the pride of Arcadia. Roseville is too small to support athletic teams but there are contests with other elementary and middle schools. The gymnasium attached to the school is larger, by far, than the school itself and it is constantly used for basketball and other game practice. Athletics are important and athletes are cynosures. The football team at Arcadia has won the district championship three out of the last five years and is widely regarded as a 'powerhouse' team. The basketball team is not as prominent but it is quite competent. The athletic contests are well attended, broadcasted over the radio, and short segments appear on television. Athletic teams for girls have not attracted much attention yet, but there are opportunities for girls to participate in some sports in the high school and the middle and elementary schools as well. The major interschool sports such as football and basketball are still considered to be a male domain.

Hinterland Features Held in Common

This is the hinterland as it is lived in Wisconsin. This Wisconson hinterland is not identical with hinterlands everywhere in the United States. However, we believe that it exhibits some characteristics that are held in common by all hinterlands in this country. We have traveled through most of them and observed and interviewed people who live there. We have also examined ethnographic and community studies from New York State, the Southeast and Deep South, Alaska, Appalachia, the Mid-west, and from the far West;

we have concluded that there are some features that appear consistently. The pivotal hinterland features are also those of the traditional male laboring class — the longshoremen, steel workers, and skilled machinists among others. We will, however, confine our discussion to the hinterland as we know it and have lived it. This hinterland is populated largely by people of White, Anglo-Saxon, North European ancestry, both Protestant and Catholic, the former predominant. It is a mainstream population, in the narrow sense of the term. It is time to name its central features in the framework of the values dialogue that has been a part of our central model.

The material living forms of the hinterland appear to be highly uniform. Neighborhoods in small towns and cities throughout every part of America can be found that look so much alike, it would be difficult to determine where one was. The house types, their lawns and shrubbery, their relationship to the street, the trees shading those streets, their distribution in relationship to the business centers, and the character and disposition of those business centers themselves are all very uniform. The small towns and cities of America are not the places of greatest innovation and change. In Arcadia, most of the houses that were built in the latter part of the nineteenth century and the beginning of the twentieth are still in good condition. When new homes are built they are built along recognizable patterns with very few radical statements. And the grid-like layout of the town, the relationship of the side streets to the main streets, the flow of traffic, the density of structures and population — all these have a consistent character.

But it is not these material features that we regard as representative of the hinterland. We are concerned about the way people enter into the American dialogue as they go about living their lives: the way in which school children are taught, the way people defend their actions, the way they comment on the outside world, the way they view political action and politicians, in short, the way they participate in the national cultural dialogue. The value orientations that are pivotal in the hinterland dialogue will be described next.

Hinterland Value Orientations

All-Around Competence

In our long-term relationships with the people and the area of Wisconsin we have described, we concluded that our friends and acquaintances did not judge us as anthropologists or university professors, but in terms of our all-around competence. When George worked with men building a house, they treated him no differently than they would treat anyone else from the neighborhood. His general construction skills were a little below par and for this he received some good natured ribbing, but they made no allowances for the fact that he was an intellectual, a professor, an author or anything other than what he was doing at the moment.

This judgment of persons in terms of their all-around competence rather than their externalized status tends to be characteristic in interpersonal relationships in this part of the hinterland. Women, too, are judged on the basis of their cooking, their house-keeping, their social skills and not on the basis of their own status or that of their husbands'.

There is, of course, danger of over generalizing. There are many people living in the hinterland who are not really hinterlanders since they came from some place else. Escapees from the city with no previous personal ties with the area carry with them their urban values and may find the behaviors and thinking of the natives a bit 'quaint' or 'different'.

The Ethic of Non-Interference

Another broad value orientation appears to be that of the 'ethic of non-interference'. There was an old woman who lived by herself on a farm that she and her husband had once operated. Her husband had died some years ago and much of the farm land had grown back into brush. Ellen lived in a rundown house with sagging screen doors and some broken windows, her barn consisted of a very old half-log structure. She had two cows to milk, (though usually one was dry), a number of chickens, among them some bantam and other relatively non-productive species, several geese, and two or three pigs. The separation between animals and Ellen was not absolute. They wandered into her house and usually stayed over night if the weather was cold. Her kitchen always had several hens roosting and frequently laying eggs on her counters and kitchen table. The calves and the pigs were moved into the basement during cold weather. We never saw the cows in the house but it does not seem impossible.

Ellen was old and sometimes not too well. She was barely making it financially and physically. She was called on by the responsible county agency to see if she should be moved into town or into a county-maintained facility. Not only did Ellen vociferously reject any such offer of help, but she received a great deal of support for this reaction from those who knew about her and her circumstances. As long as she could somehow scratch by, the attitude was she should be left alone to do so. This is generally the attitude towards individual adjustments. Unless one is harming others with one's activities, one's business is one's own, though indiscretions and peculiarities may be gossiped about.

This even expands to the regulation of activities in public areas such as lakes or streams. Some of the small lakes do not tolerate the use of large outboard motors very well. Algae is stirred up, spawning beds are destroyed, and weeds are cut up. Only with the greatest difficulty and with lukewarm support can any measures of control be exerted upon such usages. People are reluctant to interfere with the activities of others even though those activities may damage a common resource. Though a man might threaten to 'get his shotgun' when a fast boat comes too close while he is fishing, he would be most reluctant to sign a petition that might result in the implementation of some enforceable regulation.

Independence

The ethic of non-interference is closely related to the very heavy value placed upon independence. There is high regard for the independent individual who is able to work things out on his or her own, even though this independent person is expected to exist in a reciprocal relationship with friends and neighbors. The high regard for independence extends to the elderly and to young men and women as they grow old enough to 'make it on their own'.

Two Japanese anthropologists trained at Stanford University did an ethnographic study of a nearby community, Riverfront City (a town of about 18,000 population sixty miles distant). They concentrated on the care of preschool children and on the care of the elderly. They found that the teachers and caretakers of the preschool children nurtured the independence of their charges in many explicit and subtle ways. Very young children were encouraged to help themselves to food, feed themselves, and clean up their dishes when they were finished. Movements about the room, the use of toys and other facilities, and, in fact, in all areas of behavior, the emphasis on the development of independence was clear. This contrasts strongly with comparable studies that these anthropologists made of preschools in Japan. In the Japanese preschool the children are not expected to feed themselves and are not made responsible for clearing up their own debris. This is thought to be a premature requirement for very young children.

The same kinds of observations can be made about the treatment of the elderly in Riverfront City. The condition dreaded by the elderly in this town is being dependent upon one's own children for financial help, living space, or anything else on a continuing basis. They felt almost as strongly about being dependent upon community resources.

Working to Live

Another value orientation is that of working to live rather than living to work. The people around Roseville see little point to 'going away to college'. Both in Roseville and Arcadia there are many sons who are working with their fathers and will take over their father's business or farm upon his retirement. This is, in effect, a career, but is not seen in the same light as preparing to be a professional with the implications that one will move away — and almost always to a big city. The aim for most girls is still to get married and raise a family though a few years of working in an office or away from home in some service role is commonplace.

Separation of Sex Roles

This division of labor relates in turn to the separation of sex roles in the hinterland. When a group of men at a weekend social event may be standing around in the backyard drinking beer and 'shooting the breeze', and a woman steps out of the house or comes towards the group, the men fall silent and largely remain so until she withdraws. Women have their interests and these focus on the household and its maintenance and the children. If they are members of the Homemakers Club they will meet regularly to talk about improved ways of canning, preparing food, child care and other domestically-oriented activities. Many women engage in some form of artistic expression. This may be in the form of detailed handiwork such as embroidery, fancy quilting, Christmas tree decorations, pre-prepared pottery figures that can be painted in personal styles, and other activities that produce interesting and colorful objects for their homes. A few of the women become producing artists and are sometimes able to sell their pictures to others. They paint scenes from the natural environment, animals, and occasionally picturesque old buildings, such as Ellen's log barn. A few women do specialized forms of art such as Rosemaling, an intricate traditional floral design of Norwegian origin painted on wooden surfaces, frequently with messages such as *Willkommen*.

Both men and women learn from each other. The men's talk when they are alone together is not about sex, and not often about drinking exploits or fights, but rather about solving problems that they encountered in the woods or with their machinery. The anecdotes will be told in the greatest detail so that if the listeners are attentive, they will know what to do in a similar situation. There are also stories about hunting and fishing, some of which get pretty improbable. Imparting information and problem solutions likewise occurs in the women's Homemakers Meetings and in their more casual contacts when friends visit or telephone. Interpersonal relations and social networking are of more interest to women than to men.

This separation of sex roles is beginning to erode as both women and men become more conscious of women's liberation. A man who ten years ago would not have helped take the dishes off the table or bring anything to it now does so. A few men will help wash dishes, but not often, rather, they will wipe dishes. Housecleaning is almost never done by men, though a man would help out with the heavy work if it were necessary. Women, however, will quite often help out on the fields by driving tractors (as in loading hay), bringing the cows in, and in the actual milking and cleaning of stalls when the man is otherwise occupied.

There are differences between Roseville and Arcadia and even more differences between Roseville and Riverfront City. Many people in Arcadia and Riverfront City have careers, have gone to the university or local colleges and resemble their metropolitan counterparts.

Localism

Reference points for individual identities are local. The immediate locale is highly meaningful, particularly for people who are third or fourth generation in the same place. Events that took place last week, last year, ten years ago, or more, are repeated as a part of local lore. Children grow up knowing that 'the East 40 on the old Kelsoe property is where Joe cut down a tree that fell on him and almost did him in'. All of the details of how the tree fell on him, how he was saved by falling into a depression under the trunk of the tree, how he was pinned there for hours in the cold, how his wife began to worry when he didn't come home to start milking and went out to look for him, and how this could possibly happen to an experienced woodsman, are all part of the story

As an accompaniment to localism there is also the early and permanent ascription of roles and personal characteristics to individuals. These ascriptions are very hard to shake. One of our friends, for example, acquired the reputation early in life of being a little 'harum-scarum'. As a man in his middle years, this characterization 'explained' why he ran into an oak tree with his snowmobile one dark wintery night and broke his collar bone. There was less sympathy than amusement. 'You know Bill', everyone said. No matter how serious, responsible, and helpful, Bill might be (and he was), people would tend to see almost everything he did in this light. Some people move away in order to escape the roles into which they have been cast by long term public opinion.

Family and Kin

People here are also very strong on family and kin and on children. Though many people must leave this area to find work in large cities such as Chicago or Milwaukee or others along the shore of Lake Michigan, they come back for vacations and often come back to stay. Relationships are maintained no matter how far away a relative may go. When one writes a letter to an outsider, or for that matter to anyone else, most of the letter will be about what each of the children is doing, and what the condition of the husband and wife is, who has died in the immediate area, who has been born and how cousin Anne is doing in Racine.

Children are very important and most families have four or more and a few as many as ten or twelve. A couple without children is pitied and neighbors wonder what is wrong. Children are taught what their parents know and do, from their parents. They also go to school and while doing well in school is considered valuable, bookishness is not. Going away to the University at Madison or one of the branch campuses, one of them nearby at Riverfront City, is considered to be only for the quite exceptional young person who is ambitious. Ambitiousness is bound, it is felt, to draw the young person away from the local community and family and its manifestation is regarded with ambivalence. The numbers going away to college is, however, increasing.

The Dark Side

There is a darker side to the of life in this hinterland that is probably shared with other similar areas. There is bigotry, xenophobia, and in general what can be described as ethnocentrism. One woman said she could not watch the Cosby Show, which centers around a Black family, because she 'couldn't stand' to see any television program where there were a lot of Blacks. This same person, however, was generous to her neighbors, friends and family and was considered to be an individual of good character in her community.

A minister preached a sermon about 'beware of bearded strangers' when a young couple came to church. They looked somewhat like hippies; the young man had a long beard and long hair, neither of which were approved of except in very old men and hermits.

On the other hand, when the two young Japanese anthropologists came to the area to do research, they were welcomed with great hospitality. They had wondered, before they came, if they would meet with prejudice. We thought not, since one of the Methodist ministers in a nearby church was Japanese, but we warned them not to go to places where they could be mistaken for Indians. Prejudice and ethnocentrism seem to be charted along predetermined, virtually inherited, lines. The rules of hospitality and generosity overcome prejudice and ethnocentrism in individual cases, and for strangers that do not fit preconceived negatively stereotyped categories. The racism of this particular hinterland, however, does not seem as virulent as that recently surfacing on some university campuses in the United States, so racism and ethnocentrism are not necessarily distinguishing features of the hinterland. Instead they may be considered to be shared mainstream attributes found in both the hinterland and metropolitan sectors.

In general, the outside world is regarded with some suspicion. Of course people watch television and even in the poorest farmhouse there will be a large television. People watch the antics of Californians and other 'non-hinterland' groups with amusement and sometimes hostility — as in stories about street gangs in the inner city, marches asserting gay rights, or student sit-ins. On the other hand, there is a flood of images coming from the TV, so the viewers are constantly aware that the outside world holds many alternatives that are not available in the hinterland. This is the magnet that draws many young people away, but some do return, and many never leave.

Hinterland / Metropolitan Contrasts

The description that we have given of hinterland value orientations has not considered the dialogue in which these orientations are caught. Some inferences may be drawn from what has been said about the television set as a source of variant images, but there is more to this dialogue than that. The metropolitan way of life of the middle and upper-middle classes stress certain orientations that are in conflict with those previously described. Those conflicts will be outlined.

But first, it is important to understand that there is no absolute or sharp division between what we have labelled 'hinterland' and what we are calling metropolitan. Metropolitan types exist in the hinterland and hinterlanders exist in urban contexts. Small towns like Arcadia do have some individuals with metropolitan orientations living there. They tend to be professionals and business people who have come to Arcadia to practice their profession or business and who have been socialized elsewhere. Although these points have been made clear in previous discussions, they are important to keep in mind as we proceed.

Pivotal Metropolitan Values

The major thrust of upper-middle class metropolitan value orientations, constituting motivations in everyday behavior and in life choices, appear to center on a career and success within a highly competitive framework. A number of characteristics flow from this one central orientation.

The metropolitan orientation is future-oriented. Most of the time people within this context are planning for the future, thinking about the future, and worrying about the future, for themselves, for their children, even for the community, the country, or the human race. No plateau of satisfaction exists in such a framework because what is coming must be an improvement over whatever is or has been. This principle applies to corporate profits as well as to individual successes.

The future orientation is linked very closely to the career orientation. One starts planning for a career as a very young person — usually somewhere in the high school years but often before then. Many follow parental experience and goals, but some strike out entirely on their own. Planning, connected with career development, and entailing advanced education and special experience, is a special earmark of the metropolitan upper-middle class orientation.

Specialization is also a characteristic of the metropolitan orientation. Careers largely depend upon specialization, particularly professional careers. The more expert one can become in a certain line of work the more respected one will be. Within the metropolitan context, one can be a complete fool about carpentry, roof repairs, and other practical matters which are of great value in the hinterland, if one is good at one's profession. Excelling in one's profession not only compensates for incompetence in other areas, but for outright transgressions of the social code, as long as 'professionalism' is not jeopardized.

The metropolitan, career and future-oriented individual is also a highly disciplined person. These disciplines are internal and can create considerable stress. The successful, future-oriented career individual cannot externally submit to emotional stress or personal threat. This self discipline extends to health management, body care, grooming, demeanor, social relations, technical skills and personal relations. This is the ideal and is frequently violated in reality. This metropolitan type is particularly subject to the use of alcohol and other drugs to alleviate stress and depression. Stress is a common problem and a major cause of depression, hypertension, ulcers and other disorders. Stress must be managed and concern about its management contributes to the person's level of stress. The person essentially worries about worrying.

This cultural orientation requires considerable skill in self-presentation.

One must be aggressive enough to be sharply competitive but, simultaneously, one must be skilled in avoiding direct confrontations, and exert strong control over any tendencies toward aggressive displays. Academic communities are particularly negative about any physical expression of aggression. In instances where they have been outbreaks of direct aggression, even verbal aggression, the penalties have been severe. More than one academic career has been blighted by the censure levied as a consequence of such behaviour. In one instance a popular tenured senior professor who told the president of his small college to 'go to hell', in public, was penalized by a serious reduction in salary, and nearly pressured out of the institution, despite his tenured status. Minor displays of temper have caused tempests in which deans and provosts have become involved in attempts to settle out of court. Faculty meetings are often stages for skilled, and covert, but almost never overt, hostile exchanges between faculty members. Everyone acts as though he or she didn't know what was going on. Though the business world is perhaps not quite so horrified by aggression as the academic world, nevertheless aggressive emotional displays and particularly any displays of physical aggression are not sanctioned and viewed with disapproval.

The successful upper-middle class metropolitan type must be keenly competitive and successful as an expert but must also be socially well-liked. This entails being skilled at social manipulation and at hiding motives and hostile feelings; the individual is placed in a double bind. Much of the stress experienced by these persons stems from this double bind — successful competition requiring tightly controlled aggression versus sociability and popularity.

The metropolitan orientation is also low in regard for kin, family, and children. The successful younger model, the DINK, or the DIOK, 'double income no kids', 'double income one kid', is prototypical. There is a paradox here in that their way of life seems hedonistic rather than future-oriented. Although people with 'metropolitan' attitudes plan for the future, this planning tends to be very self-centered and may exclude planning for family expansion or relatives. The individual in this orientation tends to be isolated from family relationships and often from meaningful long-term relationships of any kind.

The metropolitan orientation tends to be unisex in social relations and ideology. Women are expected to carry on conversations about the same topics men do. Men are usually discouraged from gathering in small groups talking about the solutions to various technical problems or telling dirty jokes. There is presumed parity in responsibilities in the outside world and in the inner world of the home. Of course these expectations are, like all expectations, frequently unmet. Sometimes sexual parity is more apparent than actual. At parties all-male groups may form and become almost professional seminars, the counterpart of the experience-oriented anecdotes of the hinterland males. A woman who is an expert in the same area may be admitted to the group but its tenor will usually change. Sometimes women, too, constitute small conversational groups where there is talk about the problems of being a female in the late twentieth century, including the conflicts between their careers and the desire for a family.

This orientation is not constrained by locality, although there are regional and local differences. Some people develop strong attachments to a certain city or area, like 'the Bay Area' surrounding San Francisco. One's adult character is not permanently ascribed in childhood or adolescence, but is acquired and reinforced by one's behavior as an adult in whatever business and social role one is cast at a given time. People can escape their identities by changing locations, or even circles of acquaintances.

There is little 'neighborliness' in this context. The *workplace* tends to become the neighborhood as well as the family. One's most meaningful relationships with others may be found in the workplace. This situation makes it difficult for married couples to stay in contact with each other since each is primarily oriented to his or her workplace and the 'family' there. Emotional, social, and personal approbation and reinforcement may be found in the workplace instead of at home. The home is frequently just a place to stay for a little while between forays into the significant world outside. One lives in an apartment or even in a surburban detached house, separated from other people by only a few feet, but not in any form of significant personal or social contact with them. Relationships within the house or apartment may be nearly as distant. Meaningful relations are instead found in the workplace or in contacts with other professionals or business people nationwide or even worldwide.

The discussion so far can be summed up with a chart (Figure 8.1) contrasting hinterland values versus metropolitan ones, much in the same way as the traditional Menominee and mainstream cultures were contrasted. It must be understood that we are focusing on relatively extreme typologies. The hinterland type that we are talking about is real; there are individuals that live and think this way. The statements made about them are grounded in observation, but the description of the hinterland orientation does not cover the whole range of characteristics exhibited by the population of the hinterland area. An ideal type is described. The metropolitan orientation that we have described is also lived by real people in real places, but they do not constitute the whole urban middle class population. There are individuals like those described above in many places in America, but they tend to be found more often in metropolitan contexts — arbitrarily, cities of a population of 30,000 — than anywhere else. They are also upper-middle class but not necessarily WASP, though White Anglo-Saxon, North European origins dominate this group. They are individuals, irrespective of ethnicity or social class origins, who behave in the ways described.

Figure 8.1   Contrast Between Hinterland and Metropolitan Values

HINTERLAND	METROPOLITAN
General overall competence	Highly specialized expertise
Work to live — Family-oriented	Live to work — Career-oriented
Future oriented planning less developed on individual basis	Future oriented planning
Low career orientation	High career orientation
Localism	Locale more or less irrelevant
Family and kin most important	Orientation towards the professional or business workplace and relations extending elsewhere; Family and kin of lower importance Individual achievement of highest significance
Children highly valued	Children valued but often regarded as an interference with personal achievement, pleasure, and self development
'Neighborliness' and reciprocation in services and exchange of materials and time	'Neighborliness' irrelevant Reciprocation within business or professional framework important but frequently calculated
Personal characteristics and roles permanently ascribed in youth	Manipulated self presentation and role acquisition
Egalitarian	Highly individualistic, competitive orientation
Internal discipline but not as related to individual achievement and personal success	Internal discipline as related to profession, career, and social relations
Ethic of noninterference	Unclear ('Causes', such as the preservation of wilderness areas, saving endangered wildlife, stopping pollution, preventing potentially destructive development, etc. may interfere with the activities and purposes of others. Direct interpersonal interference however may be limited.)
Separation of sex roles but in enterprises such as farming, women may cross over into men's roles	At least lip service to sexual parity and blurring of sex role expectations. Male solidarity is somewhat underground

There are many ways, of course, in which hinterland Americans and metropolitan Americans are the same, particularly concerning a broad middle to upper middle class population in both areas. It is very difficult however, to make viable comparisons across presumed class lines for upper-middle class or middle class because these delineations do not mean quite the same thing in the hinterlands as they do in the metropolitan context.

We have largely ignored ethnicity in our discussion of the hinterland. In the Roseville-Arcadia area, the vast majority of the population is White and predominantly Protestant, with a sizeable Catholic minority. In the Appalachians, the Piedmont, area of North Carolina and the agricultural areas of the Mid-west, including the Southern 'Bible Belt', the population is predominantly WASP. The same is true of the hinterland areas of the West except in the Southwest, whose minorities have been partially detailed in Chapter 2. It is in the metropolitan areas where both the WASP and 'ethnic' upper-middle class strivers are encountered. There is a dynamic mix of ethnicity, though this mix is represented by a minority of persons in the metropolitan type we have described.

Our discussion has not paid direct attention to the rural Black population of the Southern US. The rural Black population has receded in significance since the great exodus from the South just prior to, during and just after World War II. On the basis of ethnographic and community-based literature on the rural South, one can conclude that some of the characteristics assigned to the hinterland culture are also characteristic of rural Blacks, but that there is a special flavor to that culture and in some ways there is a significant deviation. The Hispanic hinterland population of the Southwestern US may also be considered a significant deviation, though exhibiting many features in common. A discussion of these differences extends beyond our focus in this analysis, but they are significant. Our analysis has cast the hinterland and metropolitan typologies described as major sectors of the American mainstream. The conflicts between the two are a part of the American cultural dialogue; the conflicts within individuals in both of these sections are also a part of the dialogue.

A Hinterland School

Schools and schooling appear in many forms in the United States and it may seem futile to pick one school as representative of anything but itself. We have observed in schools on the American West Coast and in Europe. We have observed in schools in small towns, in villages, in metropolitan contexts and through the eyes of colleagues and students in the inner city; we have observed multi-ethnic schools and schools where ethnicity is homogeneous.

We will describe a relatively homogeneous school in the hinterland area of Wisconsin which was previously discussed. The Roseville Elementary School (kindergarten through eighth grade) was picked for study partly because we were familiar with the Roseville area through prolonged contact, and because we were looking for a school and environment that would be comparable to the school we had studied in the village of Schoenhausen, in Germany. We had carried on research in Schoenhausen in 1967, 1977, 1981, and at the time we started the Roseville school study (in 1983) we were planning to go back to Germany (and did) in 1985. In both schools, our focus was on schooling as cultural transmission. There are, of course, many other places in which culture is transmitted, such as the family, the church, peer groups, and by television. However the school plays a critical role as it is a major mandated institution responsible for the transmission of culture.

The Schoenhausen school and the Roseville school are matched in respect to the size of the school district, the ages of the children taught, the general curriculum, and even in the ethnic dimension, since the Roseville population is of predominantly German origin. Our selection of these two sites for study, however, is based upon one other major criterion: neither school should include a highly diversified ethnic population. We are interested in the transmission of Germanic culture in a school in a relatively rural area of southwest Germany that does not have a large guest-worker (*Gastarbeiter*) non-German population (such as the Turks that came to western Germany to work in factories and construction after WWII) and in the same sort of school in the United States: one that is ethnically homogeneous and represents a traditional hinterland mainstream orientation.

Further experience in both Germany and in the United States suggests that the behavior patterns and assumptions we discovered in both school settings are represented, to some degree, in schools everywhere in the two countries, even though there are regional and rural-urban differences. These understandings should be kept in mind while reading the description of the Roseville elementary school.

Mrs. Schillerman's Room

We entered the room at 10:15 am to observe Mrs Schillerman's combined class of first and second graders (aged 6–8).When we entered, one child was reading to a small group in a back corner of the room. The four children in the group were paying close attention to the reading. The reader turned out to be a second grader who had volunteered to read a story to some of the first graders.

Another group of children were working at their desks on arithmetic exercises prepared previously by the teacher and issued on mimeographed sheets. We later discovered that these were children who had already worked with Mrs Schillerman in a small group on exercises similar to the ones that they were now working on individually. In the front of the room, Mrs Schillerman was teaching another group on reading clocks and adding and subtracting times of day. She had a large plastic clock with red hour and minute hands that she manipulated to different times, calling for the correct time from the group and explaining problems in time-telling.

All of the children worked quietly, moving about from one place to another in the room as necessary, occasionally interrupting the teacher to ask a question or get some help on a problem. The apparent self-control of the children was very impressive and Mrs Schillerman appeared to assume that that is the way things would be.

At 11:30 there was a lunch break and the children moved in single file from the room very quietly and without any pushing or shoving. They went to the gymnasium where folding tables had been set up. Each one picked up a tray and went through the lunch line, receiving some boiled peas, french fries, small pieces of Swiss steak and a bowl of fruit gelatin. At the end of the line they received a half-pint carton of whole milk and a straw. This was all accomplished very quietly and even the talking among the children was subdued. They went to their places at the tables designated for first and second graders, sat down quietly and proceeded to eat. The noise level rose a bit. After they were finished eating they went to the trash cans that had been set up and deposited paper or plastic containers and plastic forks, knives and spoons as well as any uneaten food in them. They then stacked their trays as they left the gymnasium and returned to their classroom. When they came into the room they went to their desks and resumed working on what they had been working on before lunch, simply sat at the desk relaxing, or moved about the room talking with other children. It was a quiet and orderly room, however.

The afternoon lesson began at 12:00 and concentrated on animals threatened with extinction. The first animal was the polar bear, 'Why was the polar bear in danger?' There were reading materials available, and discussion proceeded around the penetration of Canada and Alaska by oil companies, the decimation caused by the 'sport' of hunting with aircraft, interference with breeding, and human attitudes towards large and potentially dangerous animals such as polar bears. The next animal to be discussed was the eagle, particularly the golden eagle and its endangered status. The categories of discussion were much the same and there was an interplay between prepared written materials that could be read aloud, and discussion. Interspersed with the lessons on polar bears and eagles were references to local animals such as the black bear, the deer, snowshoe rabbits and Wisconsin eagles. The differences between wild and domesticated animals were discussed, with the teacher posing questions to the children who would then answer, often posing new questions.

No opportunity was lost to make the lessons relevant to the local environment. All such discussions were open and moved at a good pace, sometimes with humorous incidents brought in. For example one child said that skunks were threatened by extinction because they 'stinct' so much!

Not only were animals in the local habitat and on the farms used as examples in discussion, but no opportunity was missed for expression of values. Cruelty to animals, the need for care for domesticated animals, moral injuctions against needless taking of animal life, were all at one point or another inserted appropriately in the flow of ideas and examples. The regulation of local hunting by game laws to preserve the local species of game animals was discussed.

Other opportunities for expressions of values occurred as children used materials, got up from their chairs, interrupted the teacher, worked with each other, and went to the closets to secure materials for individual work through the afternoon. Neatness, orderliness, self-discipline, proper use of materials, avoiding waste, considerate treatment of each other and the teacher, getting one's work done, were all stressed more than once.

When Mrs Schillerman was interviewed about her teaching philosophy and method, we asked her how she prepared the children to be so orderly and self-disciplined about the way they went about their individual and group tasks. She answered,

> I'm not sure that I do prepare them. But first of all, they must trust me and we then can develop a relationship. But trust must happen first. The children really want to do these things and they want to help each other. Some children need more help and others want to help them. I play on the positive. I praise them, 'you're very good at Math' or 'you are always so neat about your work'.

We then asked her what her underlying objective as a teacher was and she replied, 'to teach them to be an individual — to be the best they can — within the limits of that person. And I also try to help them to be a happy person'.

We asked her how the children knew just what they were supposed to be doing at any given time. She responded,

> Well, the educators (professionals from the university and school district) would like us to do more, to accomplish more in the classroom, but we have to gear what we do to the children. We try to give them a chance to exercise their own choices. They will ask,

'can we do the flashcards?' 'can we teach from the charts?'. They're all little teachers and they can make their own choice of friends to work with or teach. I think kids are really neat. If you have high expectations for them and let them know that, 98 per cent of them will meet your expectations.

One day when she had to leave the classroom for a minute, some of the children were a little bit noisier than usual. As observers, we did not think the noise level was very high but when the teacher returned she said she was 'very disappointed'.

I had an important phone call to answer and you couldn't be still for five minutes. I feel really badly about this. I went out of the room with a room filled with first and second graders but I came back to find kindergartners.

We asked her about this incident and she said,

I stress how it hurts me personally. They like me. And they feel, 'We can't hurt our teacher'. Now when I did the same thing today when I came back they had finished the page that I had assigned and they kept right on going. When I came back in and it was so lovely I praised them. I said, 'It was really nice that I could count on you and come back to such a quiet class.' They all learned.

Mrs Schillerman went on to explain that she came from a 'teaching family'.

All my sisters are teachers. I have my own philosophy. I don't feel that the children have to do every one of the worksheets that I hand out. These children don't have many friends because they live on farms rather isolated from each other and they shouldn't have to stay in to work to finish the worksheets. They need this socialization. I try not to be a grouch. Maybe some teachers think I am a little lax. I'm not really strict. I'm only a little nervous when people (like supervisors or special service people from outside), come into my classroom.

We observed all of the other classes in the Roseville School and found that although there was variation in strictness there was a great deal left up to the students themselves and they made choices consistent with the educational aims of the teachers. Furthermore, all of the classrooms were very orderly, and the children well disciplined. The discipline appeared to come from within and not be imposed by external authority. The principal of the school, Mr McNickle, said,

We don't try to be authoritarian but we try to get the children to realize that if they are disorderly and noisy all of us suffer. They are good kids and they will do their best if we let them and help them.

The contrast with the Schoenhausen elementary school was very impressive. The main difference centered upon the processes of control. In the German school, the authority imposed upon children tends to be external to them. When this authority is released for any reason the children virtually explode. They yell, run around, wrestle, and jump off and on tables. This is not considered to be bad behavior by the German teachers who say, in effect 'children will be children'. When we showed films of the Roseville school to the Schoenhausen teachers, they were very impressed with the quiet order and diversified activities in the American classrooms, but they said, 'It would never work here!' The emphasis is upon getting work done, on *Leistungsfahigkeiten* or productive efficiency, and not on self control, orderliness, or cooperation.

The Roseville school seemed to promote an idealistic concept of self-discipline, the exercise of personal choice, and individual development. These values are a part of the continuing national heritage and national dialogue. They appear in relatively pure form in this school, but they are present in some form in all of the schools we have visited in America.

Input from Outside

There are other forms of cultural dialogue in the Roseville school than those we encountered in Mrs. Schillerman's classroom. The school library has more than 5,000 books and buys about 150 new titles each year, all classified by the Dewey Decimal System and accessible through the card catalog that all children can use by the time they are in the third grade. There are also five sets of encyclopedias, several dictionaries, almanacs, atlases, a computer, numerous tapes and instructional video programs. The materials available revealed a wide range of content, sources, and age-graded media. The travelling library also comes through every Friday to bring new periodicals and books for children and professional literature for teachers. Roseville School was in no sense deprived or isolated with respect to the flow of ideas and data available to children in other American settings, including the more favored ones.

Another form of dialogue is brought to the school by special services professionals from the superintendent's office. For example, a guidance counselor appeared one day while we were observing Mrs. Schillerman's room. She took over one hour of the day's instruction to present a message about 'Letting off Steam'. This young woman, trained as a professional counselor, was concerned with 'What do you do when you're nervous? When you're under stress? When you are tired of something?'

She addressed the class, 'Didn't you feel tense when you did the Christmas program last night?' The Christmas program, put on every year and participated in by all grades is the high point of the season's celebrations and involves a great deal of work and attention on the part of the students, teachers, and administration. It is attended by all of the parents, most relatives and friends of the children in school and is a truly impressive occasion. Each grade develops and presents its own program, always in costume, and always with a great deal of color and activity.

Half of the children in the group said 'Yessss' while the other half said 'Noooooh'. The counselor said 'You wouldn't want to do it again would you?' The children seemed quite confused about this and a few tentatively muttered yes and a few muttered no, but most looked at her querulously.

She continued the theme of tension and what to do about it, 'How do you let out steam?' She showed them a book of a Black father and his son jogging: 'This is one way to relax. But what do *you* do when it's winter like this and you need to let off steam?' One child responded, 'You could dunk your head in a snow bank!'. 'What else?' said the counselor. Another child answered, 'You could shovel off all the snow!' The teacher said, 'Yes, that would be a good way to let off steam'.

Several other points were covered: whom you would ask if you wanted to find out something or you had a problem, how you would relax if there wasn't any snow to shovel, and how you could avoid 'letting off steam' on other people when you are frustrated and tense. The implication was clear that you defuse and work out all frustrations and feelings of failure by diversionary activities. Shoveling snow seemed to make some sense to these predominantly rural single-farm children in the hinterland area, but jogging didn't seem to ring any bells. Since most of them had never seen a Black they possibly concluded that only Blacks jog.

After the discussion the counselor presented the children with DUSO which was a green alligator hand-puppet. 'And what does DUSO mean?' the counselor asked. The children were not too sure, and said various things a little half-heartedly until the counselor said in a lilting voice 'Developing Understanding of Self and Others!' She went on to say that, 'DUSO is good and soft and so we hug him'. She then asked the children to line up so that each one of them in turn could hug DUSO. They proceeded to do this, some with puzzled expressions on their faces, some apparently amused and a few expressing, it seemed, a need to hug something that was good and soft.

The dialogue entering into the everyday dialogue of Roseville School from this young counselor seemed to come from a different frame of reference. Her message was how to handle emotional problems that seemed to be generated more from within an urban than a rural or hinterland framework. The idea of developing understanding of one's self and others seems psychologically sound, given certain assumptions about how people relate to each other, but the message and the dialogue within which it was embedded seemed to anticipate a way of life and the problems encountered within it that were intended to move children out of their existing lifestyle into another.

It was difficult to ascertain what the children learned, whether they internalized it, and whether it would be of use to them at this tender age. Their responses seemed, to us, to be a bit on the sardonic side. They would respond with 'yessssss' when 'no' would seem to be the obvious answer, and vice versa, or with a mixed chorus in which yes's and no's drowned each other out.

The Roseville teachers respect the people from the central district office and are grateful for the help that they receive from specialists in reading, computers, art, music and other areas. Whatever the effect of DUSO's penetration into the Roseville School dialogue, it was clearly from an outside source, but must be regarded as a part of the total dialogue experienced by the Roseville school children.

Conclusion

We have presented a case for two major forms of mainstream American cultural dialogue, one of them the metropolitan upper-middle class career-oriented dialogue and the other the hinterland. Both of them must be considered to be 'ideal types'. The specifics of cultural dialogue as they are engaged within a broad mainstream framework will be found somewhere within the general dialogue delineated by these two contrastive sets. Although the two sets seem quite different there are many qualities that are shared. The emphasis upon the individual, upon personal independence, success through hard work, a generalized optimism about the future, the value placed upon equal opportunity, and a concern about being well liked and sociable are all present but accentuated and combined in different ways in the two dialogues.

We have also described schooling as cultural transmission in the hinterland context and anticipated in Chapter 6 the schooling process in a more urban, metropolitan environment. This concludes the major portion of the analysis by George and Louise Spindler. The next two chapters are written by Henry Trueba, representing the Chicano experience with the American cultural dialogue, and Melvin Williams, representing the Black experience.

Notes

Roseville appears in two articles by G. and L. Spindler (1987a and b). Riverfront City, Wisconsin, has been studied by two Japanese anthropologists, Toshiyuke Sano and Mariko Fujita. Sano's dissertation (1989) has been completed. Sano and Fujita are presently writing a case study of Riverfront City. Some of the hinterland studies we have examined include Berry (1977), Clinton (1973), Fujita and Sano (1988), Esman (1986), Gillin (1955), Hatch (1979), Hicks (1976), Hostetler and Huntington (1976), Johnson (1975), Kunkel and Kennard (1971), Labarre (1962), Least Heat Moon (Trogdom) (1982), Perin (1977), Peshkin (1978), Sano (1989), Tauxe (1988), Vidich and Benman (1958), Vogt and Albert (1966), West (1945). Pilcher (1972), and Applebaum (1981) provide ethnographies on two working class groups — longshoremen and construction workers, respectively. The observations concerning a relevant analysis of corporate gamesmanship is provided by Maccoby (1976). The observations concerning independence in the Japanese preschool versus American, are more complex than the comparison in the text makes it. For an extended and sophisticated analysis, see Fujita and Sano (1988). They used a 'reflective' interviewing technique, developed by G. and L. Spindler (1978b) in their Roseville/Schonhausen comparison, and used videos of the Japanese and American (Riverfront City) preschools as cultural 'brackets' for the interviews.

Chapter 9

Mainstream and Minority Cultures: A Chicano Perspective

Henry Trueba

The thoughts presented here are based on my own experience in this country since 1961, as well as my experience in Mexico with Mexicans who lived in this country and returned to Mexico. These experiences are limited; consequently I cannot generalize from them alone to expand my observations. I will resort to the experiences of other Chicanos with whom I have worked, and to the Chicano literature analyzed in national and international conferences.

The National Chicano Association in its annual meetings attended by scholars from all over the world (including many Europeans and South Americans interested in American minorities — especially Hispanics) wrestles with the complex issues of identification of ethnic boundaries and membership affiliation. Their presentations are both a public celebration of cultural themes and behaviors that are characteristically 'Mexican,' as well as a source of genuine research on culture change. There is poetry in Spanish, or both in English and Spanish. There are discussions about family values, respect to the elders, folktales, and nostalgia for the homeland. There are also well-documented ethnohistorical accounts of the sacrifices of early immigrants, linguistic analyses of archaic Spanish still used in the United States, and discussions on cultural change, equity and education issues (Acuna, 1981; San Miguel, 1982, 1987). Some of the best attended presentations deal with the loss of the Spanish language, the use of 'Calo' or 'Pachuco' to express cultural experiences unique to Chicanos. At times, the Teatro Campesino or other local Chicano theater performs one of the classic representations of the cultural conflicts faced by Chicanos in North America as a result of changes in value orientation within the family.

While the discussion of mythical Aztlan as the locus of ancestral price and ethnic origin has subsided, the pride in Mesoamerican pre-colonial cultures, and the presumed cultural transmission from those early origins to contemporary Chicano community (through successive generations of Indians — our forefathers — descending from the Aztec, Mixtec, and Mayas) is still present and has become a powerful mechanism for cultural revitalization and cultural solidarity (La Raza). It takes the form of ritual consumption of alcohol in parties that start spontaneously, and of generous display of affection in a patterned Chicano way ('abrazos,' double hand shake, repeated patting on the back, and other physical and verbal expressions of affection), which translate into a renewed commitment to La Raza — to Chicanos, their culture, and their traditions.

Chicanos see no conflict between their behavior as members of mainstream society in their day-to-day professional careers, and their ethnically 'marked' behavior as Chicanos linking their existence profoundly and permanently in the Chicano community through intra-culturally prescribed interaction with other Chicanos. These behaviors are seen as perfectly compatible. Code-switching (Ornstein, 1984) plays an important function in these changes, but not the only one. Voice intonation and pitch, extended touching behavior, relative freedom to show affection to unknown Chicanos of both sexes, and joint story-telling ('chistes picantes' or 'hot jokes'), joint singing (classic 'ranchero music' from both sides of the border), among other features, signal a special within-group norm of behavior, a 'code' appropriate only for that social context, and in clear contrast with previous public interaction of same individuals.

Those attending local, national and international Chicano conferences (for example, the National Chicano Association Meetings) are primarily academicians and well-educated persons who are high achievers in American society and who have become bilingual and bicultural. Many of them stress their humble origins to emphasize their accomplishments, and some make serious efforts to regain their lost oral fluency in Spanish. They all have the conviction that there is a Chicano culture (though they argue about terminology — 'Chicano,' 'Mexican-American,' 'Mexican') which they share in common as bona fide members of the same cultural group, and that membership in this cultural group does not prevent them from functioning effectively in mainstream America. While their reports on previous and ongoing research would indicate that the process of mainstreaming for Chicanos has been slow, painful and selective, their very collective presence is a powerful demonstration of Chicano accomplishments as presidents of universities, scholars, executives, administrators, researchers, teachers, poets, community workers and aides.

Both the recognized racial and socio-economic heterogeneity and the cultural unity of Mexican immigrants is reflected in the Chicano population today. There is indeed a differential mainstreaming pace for Mexican immigrants, but there is also a strong cultural bond keeping them together.

During periods of intensive economic instability and political turmoil in Mexico, we have seen an increase in middle class Mexican immigrants along with an almost desperate escalation of rural and lower income (mostly illegal) immigrants (McCarthy and Burciaga, 1985, 1986; US Department of Commerce, 1987). Their successful and rapid adaptation to mainstream America is contingent upon a number of factors, including educational level and relative exposure to modern technological metropolitan areas. Most rural Mexican immigrants go through a longer period of transition and adaptation in comparison to their urban counterparts.

The Chicanos who are viewed as well-adjusted mainstreamers, bilingual, bicultural, perfectly competent citizens functioning effectively in all existing public social institutions, are also those who promote Chicano culture and the Spanish language. Some of them have married Anglo-Saxon spouses, but have retained a bicultural environment in their home, without becoming disenfranchised (McCarthy and Burciaga, 1985, 1986; Trueba, 1988a). In contrast, many recent Mexican immigrants feel the pressure to acculturate and to abandon their language and culture. An example of efforts to comply with this pressure is the majority Hispanic vote on Proposition 63 in California — the English-Only Proposition supported by 59 per cent of Hispanics in the state, in contrast with the position adopted by well-educated and more liberal non-Hispanic persons, by the Police and Fire Departments, and by other public office personnel (Trueba, 1989).

How do Chicanos view themselves and those from the 'mainstream society'? What is their perception of the American culture and values? How do Chicanos view the rights of the individual, freedom of speech, equality, social mobility and achievement through hard work, and how do we as Chicanos view ourselves collectively in the broader national context? How do we view schools and our children's performance? There are significant differences within Chicano groups with respect to their internalization of stress asssociated with the pursuit of 'success' and 'high achievement' as understood by the middle and upper class professionals. In general, many professional Chicanos spend most of their professional lives with mainstream, competitive Americans, and consequently feel equally oppressed by demands to achieve and to dramatize their achievement through conspicuous consumption — demonstrated, for example, in the purchase of expensive cars and homes. They feel torn apart from traditional family values and show signs of guilt in displaying conspicuous consumption expressed in the form of hyperexplanations to friends and relatives, in large contributions to family and community causes, in generous demonstrations of hospitality to relatively unknown lower income relatives and friends.

While Chicano professionals are seen by mainstream peers as 'doing well,' competing successfully, some may be seen by Chicano peers as greedy, materialistic and insensitive to the needs of the mass of poor Chicanos. The result of these conflicting messages is an ambivalence about economic success, and efforts to decrease conspicuous consumption and to invest in charity with less fortunate Raza. There is, however, in the minds of Chicanos a struggle between displaying total independence from Chicano family and friends (viewed as necessary to function effectively in mainstream society) and a certain dependence on Chicano family and community as sources of identity and satisfaction. As a successful Chicano, one must keep a delicate balance between pride, success, conspicuous consumption, and humble membership in the lower income Chicano family and community, with consistent and controlled dependency on both, and through systematic investment of some resources. A good Chicano, no matter how successful and rich, must always share wealth and success, information, support and affection with the less fortunate 'carnales y carnalas' (brothers and sisters), and with their 'jefitos y jefitas' (dear parents). Recent research shows the powerful force that the family has on the lives of Hispanic immigrants (Alvarez, 1988; Suarez-Orozco, 1989).

In previous chapters George and Louise Spindler have described the difficulties in defining mainstream and minority cultures. Some individuals whose membership in the American mainstream culture is assumed by most WASP persons see themselves as members of minority groups. This occurs in spite of the fact that neither minority nor mainstream people would classify them as minority. In contrast, some minority persons want to 'pass' for mainstream and spend much of their lives attempting to be accepted as members of the mainstream American society, despite the fact that everyone else sees them as minority. (The literature on 'passing for' in the context of minority literacy is discussed by Rueda and Mehan, 1986). Who is then mainstream, and who is minority? Can we choose our affiliation? As in any ethnic or cultural groups, there seems to be a spectrum of differential membership and differential affiliation for minority groups that may extend to individuals only marginally associated with the minority group. Indeed we hold flexible operational definitions and criteria for ethnic identification, and manipulate boundaries in diverse political contexts. Many Chicanos classified (by others and themselves) as mainstream pursue an ethnic identification by using their Spanish first names rather than their English first names, by associating with other Chicanos and even by adopting the use of Spanish in informal conversations.

Minimal Surface Characteristics of Mainstreamers

In accordance with this text and the work of the Spindlers published elsewhere (G. Spindler, 1977, 1987a, 1987b; G. Spindler and L. Spindler,

1983, 1987) I would consider a mainstream American person (regardless of ethnohistorical background) as one who:

— Is fluent in English with a native-like oral skill.
— Has internalized the values traditionally viewed as 'American' which were discussed by the Spindlers in Chapter 3.
— Participates meaningfully in American social, political, and economic institutions.
— Consciously accepts mainstream affiliation as part of his/her personal identity.

If we were to take the operational criteria described above, we would not consider as mainstreamers lower income, isolated, marginalized, socially outcast persons (even if they are Whites), but we would classify as mainstreamers some Italians, Blacks, Chicanos, Indians, and other descendants from immigrant minorities, provided they fulfill the four criteria stated above, in spite of the fact that they retained some degree of affiliation with non-mainstream cultures. Mainstreaming is impossible when a person or group is willingly or unwillingly kept in isolation (social, cultural and economic). But in circumstances of having free access to American mainstream society, immigrant, refugee and other minority people can become members of mainstream society without cutting their ties with their original minority culture. This is obtained by becoming bilingual or even bicultural, and by acquiring the linguistic, cognitive and cultural knowledge and skills necessary to function effectively in mainstream public social institutions.

Membership in mainstream and/or minority groups is ascribed on the basis of physical, linguistic (primarily phonetic) and behaviorial characteristics. Cultural attribution (the collective ascription of ethnic or mainstream membership on the basis of superficial characteristics) may be in conflict with cultural affiliation (one's own ethnic identity as internalized by each individual). Collective perception of membership is particularly painful to individuals who share characteristics and cultures viewed as incompatible and resulting from intermarriages perceived as undesirable. For instance, when Black or White Americans married Vietnamese women, their offspring were low-status and stigmatized 'Amerasians' in Vietnam, Laos or Thailand, a stigma that was drastically reduced or even disappeared as these children were recognized as 'Americans' and accepted in the US.

The very elastic nature of ethnic affiliation functions as a solution to culture conflicts. Professional Chicanos can be competitive, successful, independent, yet humble, respectful of family and community, and generous. A monolithic, monocultural ethnic affiliation to either Chicano or mainstream culture is not necessary (Rueda, 1987; Trueba, 1989).

Chicano vs. 'Mainstream American Culture'

Using my experience in the Chicano and Mexican communities, and their notions of cultural affiliation/attribution, I want to discuss Chicano perspectives on American mainstream culture (its tenets, values, philosophy and day-to-day reality), cultural conflicts, and their implications for schools.

Working with Chicano students and faculty and establishing a close relationship with them and their families brings the realization that some of the Mexican cultural values (often identified with the rural life of pre-arrival experiences) continue and become integrated into the daily life of Chicano professionals. I will enumerate a few of these values:

— Generous hospitality which includes food, shelter and other necessities to relatively unknown Chicanos or Mexicans, without expectation of personal reciprocity.
— Family organization in which parents continue to occupy a place of high respect and authority even after children have grown up and have become independent.
— Informal networking (often based on blood and/or real and fictitious kinship ties) for reciprocal emotional, social and economic support.
— Distrust of the impersonality of the social system and public institutions, and reliance upon personalized relationship with public service personnel.
— Profound adherence to religious beliefs acquired during the early years of socialization.
— The role of women as mothers and their influence on the family is stressed, while the potential professional career of women outside the home is deemphasized.
— The role of males in the family as primary economic supporters is enhanced by the ultimate authority and disciplinary functions ascribed to them.
— A measure of stoicism in the face of hardship, as well as the strong emotional support from members of the extended family expected during major life crises and events.
— Privacy and respectful distance are viewed as the appropriate public response to the conspicuous consumption of richer folks, and to the misbehavior of other persons outside the family.
— Personal responsibility to help relatives. The more money you have the more responsible you become to help others, particularly those members of the family who still live in Mexico.
— Guilt and anxiety about signs of disloyalty to La Raza as a collectivity. For example, insensitivity to other Chicanos and

Mexicans, lack of hospitality or respect, siding with the 'Gringos,' embarrassing one's own parents, the poor or the elderly, and similar behaviors are considered the most despicable demonstration of disloyalty to one's own Raza.

Chicanos who have become academically or economically successful, seem also to have adjusted well to this country by integrating their home values with those of mainstream America (G. Spindler, 1987a, 1987b). They are often bilingual and bicultural, and tend to accommodate traditional Mexican culture values in very creative ways. They maintain close communication with their Mexican relatives, visit Mexico often, create networks around social occasions and recruit persons interested in Mexican art, music and cuisine. Mexican cultural values are not only resilient over generations, but flexible enough to permit many Chicanos the extension of their networks in both the Chicano and mainstream communities. Beyond the required linguistic skills for code-switching from English to standard or local varieties of Spanish, well adjusted Chicanos behave in ways culturally congruent with each community — the more traditional Mexican community and the well-established mainstream community — even in instances where these communities tend to be culturally incompatible or antagonistic to each other. The explanation for this phenomenon may be the ability of Chicanos to internalize both sets of values and selectively integrate them in specific interactional settings. Chicanos are outstanding in identifying a certain complementarity of values by distinguishing interactional settings and contexts. For example, Chicano home values are considered top priority in the privacy of the home or with close friends, while mainstream values are the norm for behaving in public arenas (Delgado-Gaitan, 1986, 1987a, 1987b).

Freedom of Speech and Equality

Freedom of speech in public in order to deal with issues that are socially significant, is a well-recognized and frequently used right by Chicanos. Equality as a value, if used in the public arena, is also an unambiguously defended and advocated right. Yet the concept of equality is never taken outside of the public social context and applied to personal or family relationships and values. There is clear distinction of sexual roles and statuses, and a clear authoritative role for the father. Equality in inter-ethnic settings is not discussed, but there is some ambivalence about accepting other groups on an equal basis. Cultural differences are pointed out and distinguished from the early child socialization years.

During the Civil Rights struggles of the 1950s and 1960s, the organizers of the Chicano Movement, especially the well-educated bilinguals who understood the intricacies of American history, values, and traditions, led picketings and acts of civil disobedience in support of the Cesar Chavez, Reies Tijerina and Corky Gonzalez Movements (Acuna, 1981; San Miguel, 1986). They used the university as a political forum to vent feelings of unhappiness with lack of educational opportunity for minorities, and with the incongruency between claimed mainstream American values (such as individual rights, freedom of speech, equality for all) and the social reality of indifference about minorities working in the fields for unfairly low wages and under considerable health risks. Chicanos from all social strata joined forces with political advocates of those movements, while Chicano lawyers were carrying out numerous lawsuits in response to discrimination practices in employment, education and public service in Texas, California, New Mexico, Colorado and Arizona. While many of these lawyers had already become mainstreamed (judging from their life styles and professional statuses), their renewed loyalty to La Raza demonstrated profound cultural roots and devotion to their ancestors and the causes of contemporary Chicano communities. This is a clear case of cultural revitalization characterized by the intensive search for cultural experiences left behind years before.

When I was teaching in Sacramento State University in the early 1970s I was invited by other Chicano faculty to get up at 4:00 am and to join them in the 'desayuno para los niños' 'breakfast for children' in a downtown barrio. The entire family of one of the faculty was responsible for buying materials and preparing breakfast for several hundred young children, while others assisted serving it to children and cleaning up afterwards. It became a major operation that lasted several years and it was financed by contributions from many Chicanos in business and professional careers.

What kept La Raza together during those years of Civil Rights struggles was an intensive and profoundly meaningful experience of sharing the cultural values referred to above. In the hot late spring afternoons of Sacramento, Chicanos from various local organizations used to convoke informal art festivals with exhibitions of popular art in a public park near the State University. Barbecued ribs and drinks were offered to all who attended, while poets, musicians and the public performed. In the context of a happy inter-ethnic audience, these local poets, musicians and their apprentices would capture the heart of the audience and invite participation from all. The code-switching in poems and songs, the tears and laughter in response to the vivid description of the fears, tragedies and conflicts faced by La Raza, and the final demonstration of mutual affection are unforgettable. They laughed at the 'Chota' (police) and the 'Migra' (immigration patrol), and at the Chicanos pretending to behave like Anglos, 'passing for' mainstream. It was a way of releasing their anxieties and re-interpreting tragic moments of their lives associated with their cultural conflict, and symbolized by their alternate use of English, Spanish and barrio 'Calo.' The performers skillfully illustrated the misunderstanding, unmet expectations, confusion and traumas of recent immigrants attempting to understand Anglo-Americans, as well as the problems of Anglo-Americans attempting to communicate with the immigrants.

The height of the dramatic representations of the cultural conflicts experienced by Chicanos was reached by the *Teatro Campesino* or *Teatro del Pueblo.* Typically, their plays touched on themes related to the brutal encounters with police or immigration officers, or the painful discovery of disloyalty to family values for the sake of 'passing for Gringo,' and the ultimate loss of Chicano ethnic identity and cultural values, such as the respect for elders, love for family, generosity and candor with Raza. In clear contrast to these values, the 'Gringo' or mainstream culture was depicted as plagued by insensitivity and materialism. One of the favored themes was that of the cultural changes in Chicano children who no longer feel accountable to their parents or part of the family, and who take social roles which place them in tragic conflict with the Chicano community.

In one play, for example, a Chicano police officer arrested his own brother, in another an immigration officer arrested his own mother and deported her to Mexico. The most powerful dramas revolved around the 'Vendido,' the 'sold' Chicano who betrayed his own Raza to become 'acceptable to the Gringo' or a member of mainstream society, and who ended by being betrayed by the members of mainstream society. There were other plays in which the 'Vendido' was a vain Chicano seeking the love of the 'Gueras,' the 'Blondes,' thus underestimating the beauty and virtues of Chicanas. He also was betrayed at the end and left isolated. Another play depicted a young child who eventually climbed to the top of economic success through the sacrifice of parents and siblings, and who abandoned his family to marry a 'Guera,' only to die tragically alone. These themes represent some folk beliefs and culturally appropriate responses to the cultural conflicts faced by Chicanos in the process of becoming part of mainstream America. Educated and professional Chicanos are still deeply affected by the *Teatro* and take seriously the profound messages of loyalty to La Raza. Their efforts to maintain both loyalty and independence, to keep their ethnic identity while at the same time achieving highly in the Anglo competitive world, result in the bicultural compromises alluded to earlier. They will find opportunities to share their wealth, knowledge and support to help low-income Chicanos. They will participate in barrio-type parties where there is a conspicuous absence of the status symbols either in clothing, or in expenditure. Parties in public parks, schools, art centers, community centers, offer opportunities to professionals to share with the poor, to be treated as equals (while everybody knows their professional status), to join in 'corrido' music, in the use of Spanish and Chicano dialects more familiar to the recent immigrants and non-professionals, drinking Mexican drinks (tequila, mezcal, etc.), showing affection, offering help, and extending network connections. The ultimate sign of ethnic loss is the consistent lack of participation in these activities.

Perhaps the fact that many Chicanos who become educationally and economically successful maintain a low-key profile, and quietly and smoothly pass over the ethnic line to become mainstream Americans, indistinguishable from others, may have something to do with the social sanctions attached to 'betraying' Raza. On the other hand, the incentives associated with becoming a member of the mainstream group are powerful. If one becomes successful in public life, one is treated with the status and respect given to any other member of the mainstream culture. Can a Chicano maintain in private his or her life style, networks of friends and relatives, and the Chicano value system? Many Chicanos see this as a possible integrative alternative. This approach can perhaps work most of the time, but it certainly does not work on occasions in which public action is required as a means to publicly defend the civil rights of *all* Chicanos.

The pressure from Chicano networks is such that one must engage in public action. The Chicano faculty at Sacramento State University would often convoke a private meeting to discuss joint action. In these occasions several faculty members would approach a colleague to make a specific request, such as his or her participation in, or contribution to an activity, or to present a group complaint. On one occasion, a Chicano faculty member who had disparaged another Chicano during important meetings in Washington was confronted by the entire group and warned severely. Later on this person felt compelled to seek a position in another institution.

There is a great deal of collective power and peer solidarity. But there is also sincere affection and tolerance for peers' personal weaknesses. Antisocial behavior associated with drinking is handled privately and with patience. The group comes first, sometimes at the expense of one's own family commitments. There is a feeling of profound personal loyalty and commitment to the maintenance of the group's welfare, and a commitment to personal relationships above and beyond the normal expectations in mainstream friendships.

This commitment is demonstrated in providing economic help, housing, food, emotional support and even the use of personal property for undetermined periods of time to relatively unknown Chicanos if a 'compadre' or peer requested it as a personal favor. Compadrazgo relationships served well these type of behaviors. A compadre/comadre, as it happens in old Mexico, was always entitled to this kind of support, even if he/she had already received a great deal more than given in return to anyone in one's own network.

The Process of Mainstreaming

The view of mainstream culture as compatible with Chicano culture, and the identification of particular mechanisms to integrate both cultures, are an important characteristic of well-adjusted and successful Chicanos. Through these mechanisms they have created a broad basis for the socioeconomic mobility of a number of families forming collective units that I have called 'networks' here (Velez-Ibanez and Moll, 1989). They include not only blood relatives and members of the kin, but compadres and friends.

One could speculate that pursuing upward social mobility by single individuals not concerned with family welfare and cultural ties might be more expedient. But the evidence we have to the contrary is substantial. From my own experience and some studies, it is clear that, in spite of the difficulties encountered, Chicanos (and their Mexican ancestors living in this country) move up socio-economically and have done well in comparison to other immigrant groups. While the increasing numbers of Mexican immigrants create semi-permanent and sociologically visible low-income, poorly-educated Chicano communities in the southwest, the mobility of individual families and groups of families is a well-documented reality. The reports from the Rand Corporation and the studies at the University of Arizona indicate that Mexican immigrants use networks extensively to maximize economic progress, and that they have followed the same process as European immigrants have who came with little formal education and from rural areas. For them, education has been the opening of the door to employment opportunities. They and their children are increasingly obtaining more highly skilled and professional positions as teachers, managers, technicians, sales clerks, nurses, lawyers, and doctors. The role of the family network in the educational support given to children is clear. And so is the reciprocal service relationship of many Chicano professionals to the Chicano community. Education has been and still is the gate to mainstream America for Chicanos, as well as other groups, and plays a key role during the process of cultural socialization into American mainstream values.

In the process of the mainstreaming of Chicanos, that is, the process whereby Chicanos integrate their home values with those predominant in mainstream America and inculcated in schools, one could identify three major and distinct phases. The initial phase is characterized by culture shock resulting from the first encounters with the members of the dominant society outside the home and local community. The intermediate phase involves intensive peer socialization activities geared to learning how to deal with the new system, and is characterized by ambivalence about one's own cultural values and attempts to integrate them with those of the dominant society. The final phase of successful reconciliation of cultural values can open unique alternatives for bilingual and bicultural Chicanos which are never discovered by others. Additive bilingualism and biculturalism, constructive marginality and integration of values are not always the outcome. Some Chicanos end up in isolation, withdrawal, regression, long-term transitionality and disenfranchisement.

Initial Phase: Culture Shock

Many Chicanos start their life in socially and culturally isolated environments. During the early years of home socialization, whether they live in the barrio, or continuously go with their migrant parents from one place to another as they search for agricultural labor, they are always segregated in camps or low income neighborhoods. Lack of exposure to English speaking, mainstream American families deprives children of acquiring an understanding of mainstream language and culture, and the significance of literacy for social upward mobility. Younger children are often born when parents have decided to settle in one area and facilitate the education of their children. This is a decision full of economic uncertainties and risks, often demanding a difficult adjustment in the lives of a migrant family. Their annual cycle of activities takes the household back to Mexico or to places in the US where the cost of living is bearable during the long months of unemployment.

The side of America that Chicano migrant children and their families see is indeed quite different from that most other families experience. I will mention just a few that are characteristic of Chicano migrant childrens' life:

— Life of poverty and rural isolation. This means, at best, the lack of privacy in crowded and poorly insulated dwellings, lack of showers and toilet facilities, lack of comfort, and lack of regular medical services. At worst, it means child abuse, malnutrition, poor health and neglect.
— Cultural and linguistic isolation. This entails cognitive underdevelopment, educational neglect, late exposure to literacy, low school achievement, and often stereotypic classification into learning disability groups.

— Lack of appreciation for one's own culture, and lack of self-esteem. This will probably result in social and economic dependence on low-paying jobs, and low overall achievement aspirations, low income and low social status.
— Incompetence and shock in dealing with mainstream persons and representatives of social institutions such as banks, hospitals, stores, recreation facilities, churches, businesses, and service agencies.
— Serious difficulties of adults in written and oral English communication with mainstream persons. This results in the need to use migrant children (partially bilinguals) as translators, thus placing on them adult responsibilities (related to making financial and personal decisions) which children are not prepared to take.
— Deep frustration of parents in day-to-day interaction with mainstream people, and often suspicion of unfair treatment and racism. Parents' feelings and views may create in children some hostility towards, and misconception of mainstream values.

The initial phase does not affect equally all of the children in the family. Older children have burdens and responsibilities that younger children rarely face. Older migrant children describe in stronger terms their experiences working in the fields, moving around the country, living in unsanitary conditions and feeling humiliated in schools. Some children remember when their hair was washed with kerosene (an inhuman solution to the lice problem), or was cut in front of their Anglo peers. Others remember their peers calling them names and covering their noses because 'those Mexican kids smell bad'.

Previous studies suggest that the differential, often minimal participation patterns can be reduced to three main ones:

— Hypo-participation, or extreme efforts to be inconspicuous and be left alone.
— Hyper-participation, which is characterized by anxious, superficial and unproductive activities attempting to imitate others.
— Hostile/selective participation, characterized by desperate and destructive efforts to delay or prevent unpleasant participation in school activities.

For example, Rosita, a Mexican fourth grader, would keep her head down on the bench the entire class period. Sometimes she just sat there quietly, daydreaming as if she had given up entirely any attempts to make sense of the world around her (Trueba, 1988b).

We have some evidence that minority children, including Chicano children from migrant families, often go from a state of deep depression and mental isolation to a state of panic. This is shown in their decreasing attempts to participate, respond to questions, and their inability to focus on simple directives which they previously followed. There are many other signs of emotional turmoil: undefined fears, physical restlessness, unfocused gaze, uncontrolled feet and hand movements, and frequent need to go to the bathroom. These signs tend to increase during times of forced performance in front of large groups of mainstream children. These performances often result in serious embarrassment to Chicano children, especially if reprimanded for not doing well. In my fieldnotes I recorded instances in which the teacher asked specific questions about reading, math, or homework which children could not answer, and instances in which these children were asked to read in front of the class, that resulted in making them physically upset, to the point of needing to excuse themselves to go to the bathroom. Some times they would respond 'I don't know' in an angry tone that tended to discourage the teacher from asking them again. Other times they would just lower their head, show a red-faced smile of embarrassment, and remain motionless.

I still recall the case of Joaquin, a boy in the third grade in southern California who refused to be placed in the Spanish/English bilingual program, assuring everybody (despite his heavy accent) that he spoke only English, that his parents did too, and that he lived in a beautiful big house out of town. It turned out that he lived out of town but in a very small trailer with his three older brothers and mother, recently arrived from Mexico, who worked in the fields.

Intermediate Phase: Cultural Socialization

With the settling of many Chicano families in urban areas, whether this happens immediately after their arrival to the US or after several years of migrant life, the control of the parents and the maintenance of the home values rapidly disappears. Some recent studies show that newly arrived Mexican families settled in the Los Angeles area face serious disciplinary problems with their teenage children, problems that threaten family unity. Urban life seems to bring a strong influence from peer socialization and the new mainstream values as experienced in the low income metropolitan areas and through the media. Low income urban areas are usually the center for drug traffic and gang activities.

Survival, racial confrontations, inter-and intra-ethnic cultural conflicts, and sometimes sheer economic gain become major incentives for involvement in gang activities. School remains as the key agent of cultural socialization, that is, the locus of intensive exposure to mainstream values. Schooling for Chicanos is therefore characterized by keen awareness of the political processes and the use of power in American society. The following are some of the characteristics of this phase:

— Peer socialization away from the home.
— Departure from home cultural values, except when these values are actively and collectively advocated by peers outside the home.
— Economic independence (at least partial) on the part of the youngsters who earn money by legal or illegal means.
— Awareness of differential social status ascribed to ethnic groups and members of mainstream society.
— Experiences with prejudice in employment, housing, schools, churches, parks, buses, and other public places, and of feelings of resentment towards mainstream persons.
— Experience of verbal and physical violence both at home and in the community, both of pain received and pain inflicted.
— Encounters with police, legal authorities, and other public offices representatives.
— Acquisition of manipulative skills necessary to deal with the mainstream system effectively, and in attempts to bypass prejudice. Learning 'to pass for' a mainstream person.

There is a Chicano who, years ago used to drink too much, and who, crying and laughing at the same time, told me that when he was twelve years old he became conscious of his dark skin color. He used to wash his face every night with milk, and powder it in the morning with the hope of turning it into a light brown color. He used to think that if only he was 'White' he could pass for 'Gringo'.

Often within the same family children may have different tones of light brown or dark brown skin. The distribution of labor in order to beat the system and get fair treatment for all is strategized by skin color. Lighter children 'pass for Gringos' and therefore are encouraged to represent the others and help them. Pretending to be a mainstream person is a difficult operation that requires talent, observation and imitation skills for talking, walking, moving, gesturing, and acting like people out of the Chicano community do. There are Chicanos who are truly skillful and achieve a high degree of proficiency at this during their high school years. If they are not caught code-switching with another Chicano, observers might never think they were Chicanos.

Third Phase: Cultural Integration

Different Chicanos proceed at different paces in the process of reconciling Chicano and mainstream cultural values. In fact, some Chicanos go either to the extreme of totally rejecting mainstream values, or the opposite extreme of rejecting their home culture. In general, Chicanos want to view Chicano culture as an integration of Mexican values with their own values resulting from their experience in this country and their struggle with mainstream society. The blend of mainstream values in the life of Chicanos does not happen randomly.

In talking about the Menominee, the Spindlers compare and contrast mainstream with Native American behavioral attitudes and values. Chicano adaptations can be better understood with reference to the Spindler's framework of power vs. humility, individualism vs. autonomy, competitive achievement vs. quiet progress, aggression vs. latescence, folk religion vs. institutional religion, sexual repression vs. sexual freedom, constructive marginality and biculturalism vs. withdrawal, and dysfunctional compensatory adaptation.

One of the reasons why Chicano organizations have often suffered in their early stages of development is that the pursuit of power and the control of groups should not be initiated by the individual without previous request by the collectivity. Culturally, it is inappropriate to seek political power without the spiritual power or the charisma which can be recognized by the group. Service to the community, generous giving of one's own time and personal resources, personal charm and speaking ability, organizational skills coupled with low-key and humble personality, are the ways to be recognized as a leader and asked to take over power positions. Obviously it is not always the most charming individuals who have the drive and organizational skills to run Chicano organizations effectively. Even some of the Chicano professional organizations suffer today from this apparent conflict between cultural norms against conspicuous display of power, control and leadership, and the needs of the organization for its effective functioning.

The conflict between individualism or autonomy and the need for a collective identity discussed by the Spindlers is one of the most painful manifestations of the conflict suffered by transitional Chicanos. There is a great deal of individualism and autonomy in younger Chicanos in day-to-day business transactions, but major decisions regarding the acceptance of better employment opportunities which require residential change and place physical distance between the nuclear family and other immediate relatives are conducted in consultation with the members of the extended family. Often the security and support of the extended family is seen as a preferable collective good over the gains of individual nuclear families.

There are critical events that seem to trigger cultural integration, such as enrolling in the military service, travelling extensively, pursuing a higher degree or profession in competition and association with mainstream persons, marriage with a mainstream person, and similar other experiences that facilitate intensive and prolonged exposure to mainstream lifestyles. Some of the characteristics of this phase could be the following:

— Late academic intensive socialization, with a better understanding of the functional value of literacy and educational training for survival in America.
— Genuine discovery and appreciation of mainstream values within their social context, for example of the honor system, the conformity with public rules and regulations in order to act effectively as a group, individual discipline and personal reliability in socially cohesive units, the use of authority and power for the sake of the community, and the need for financial planning.
— Discovery of racial/ethnic stereotypes in day-to-day interaction with mainstream peers, both in reference to Chicano culture on the part of mainstream persons, as well as in reference to mainstream culture on the part of Chicanos.
— Need for revitalization ceremonies which bring the reaffirmation of one's own traditional cultural values into perspective, in contrast with those more recently acquired in contact with mainstream society.
— Experimentation in the use of mainstream values to bring desired effects, and partial, gradual, or experimental acceptance.
— Ability to function in mainstream circles through effective oral and written communication, and to establish personal relationships with members of the mainstream society.
— Further internalization of selected mainstream values stimulated by expected desirable outcomes such as rewards, access to resources, and recognition of one's own success.
— Contextualized commitment to abide by mainstream values in specific settings (at work, in public institutions, etc.), and under specific interactional circumstances (dealing with certain kinds of people).
— Bicultural skills to code-switch and use either set of values in different interactional arenas.
— Skills and long-term commitment to exhibit and promote mainstream values in public settings, provided certain home and community values are protected.

Chicanos spread through the continuum described by the Spindlers in Chapter 6 between competitive achievement (à la mainstream Anglo) and quiet inconspicuous competent performance (à la Menominee). Some school children have been raised in the rural cultural tradition of cooperative work and have difficulty assuming competitive attitudes (even when the competition is between groups and there is room for cooperative work within the group or family). Professional Chicanos can come across as competitive and cut-throat as any other mainstream professional in America. Yet they develop inconspicuous collaborative relationships with other Chicano professionals — *inconspicuous*, in order to avoid other peoples' suspicions of being less competitive or blinded by ethnic bonds — whereby they can fulfill cultural goals of cooperation and reciprocity.

It is culturally unacceptable in the traditional Mexican culture of most middle or low-income immigrants to the United States to show overt aggression, or to express freely and publicly personal feelings of pain, anger, jealousy, or love. With an internalization of mainstream values and the biculturalism acquired by some Chicanos, there is a concomitant increase in the free expression of feelings. However, the freedom to express feelings is contextually appropriate with other peers equally acculturated of the same generation or with mainstream persons; not with members of older generations who see such free expression as a sign of spiritual weakness, lack of control or bad manners.

One may see in one day a professional Chicano acting as a key person in mainstream organization in the morning (a top executive, lawyer, teacher, expert, or highly-skilled worker); then meeting at noon with Chicano colleagues; going home for supper in the evening; and finally attending a night community meeting in the barrio. This Chicano could probably code-switch into five different linguistic/cultural interactional styles extending from formal, standard, mainstream American in the role of institutional representative, to colloquial American and Spanish, used interchangeably without conspicuously excluding Anglo friends, to a formal Spanish in the home (with all the peculiar cultural and linguistic usages), to finally a barrio-type of Spanish (rural and mixed with 'Calo'). Along with the linguistic forms, the paralinguistic and kinetic features of the communication would clearly indicate this Chicano's ability to become a member of the mainstream, to communicate effectively with other members of the mainstream in each setting.

Assimilation of Chicanos to Mainstream Culture

Total assimilation to mainstream culture entails not only the ability to function in mainstream society, but also the loss of ability to function in Chicano settings — to have lost one's own language and culture. There is a difference between an assimilated Chicano and a bilingual/bicultural one. The home lifestyle and the values exhibited in public by Chicanos who have lost their ethnic cultural ties seem to contradict skin color and even remnants of conversational Spanish, and taste for Mexican food. Inevitably, many second and third generation Chicanos (or Mexicanos) feel compelled to assimilate into mainstream life very rapidly through a number of mechanisms.

Assimilation starts primarily by a weakening of ethnic ties and values, loss of membership in Chicano networks, and loss of contact with the Chicano extended family. The end result of assimilation is a lifestyle no different from other mainstream Americans who, over a period of years, become equally uprooted from the culture of their immigrant parents or grand-parents.

Here are some of the characteristics usually marking signs of assimilation:

— Keen awareness and priority of social class status, and active membership in middle and upper-middle social class organizations.
— Marriage into a mainstream family equally conscious of social status.
— Loss of contact with ethnic group organizations, and ethnic peers.
— Change in religious beliefs and practices; from Catholic to Protestant, or from a Fundamentalist church to a more liberal church; or from frequent church-goer to an occasional church-goer.
— Increase in educational level and career specialization.
— Decrease in social consciousness and loss of commitment to serve or assist one's own Raza, or what used to be seen as one's own Raza.
— Lastly, loss of active membership in the extended family signaled by persistent absence in life cycle crises or in major events previously attended.

Not all Chicanos feel compelled to assimilate. Some Chicano families have persisted for six or seven generations in spite of changes in language, religion and social class by many of their members. It is not clear why, excepting that the Chicano extended family continues to serve important social, economic and religious functions which are unique to the Chicano culture and can still enrich families who participate in the mainstream society. The value of the Chicano extended family is recognized by the mainstream males marrying Chicanas. Often these mainstream spouses see cultural adoption in Chicano families as a positive gain and maintain for life an active role in the extended family functions.

Not always, however, is there a happy ending in the long journey of the Chicano mainstreaming process. It is rather paradoxical that those Chicanos who anxiously seek assimilation and feel compelled to 'pass for' members of mainstream society often succeed the least in adjusting to life in the US. While they lose membership in their original ethnic group, they also fail to obtain total acceptance in the mainstream society; consequently they become long-term transitionals.

Transitional Chicanos

There is remarkable parallel between the transitional Menominee described by the Spindlers and the transitional Chicanos. It is a known phenomenon on both sides of the border that many Mexicans who lived in the United States for a long time feel accepted neither in Mexico nor in the United States. They travel periodically to and from Mexico, and are equally out of place in both countries. They essentially lose some of their values which they have not internalized. These individuals often lose control of their home language, that is, the language they learned as children, without ever reaching full control of English, their second language. They remain isolated and disenfranchised in both countries, feel insecure and vulnerable, attribute to race or skin color (their own and that of others) people's behavior which they interpret as hostile. Transitional Chicanos project resentment, and in some cases they suffer serious mental disorders. The failure and traumas associated with their desperate attempts to pass for, to belong to and participate fully in the mainstream American society, are intimately related to their failure to maintain their home language and culture, and the support system that their ethnic community offers them. The main characteristic of these individuals is a social and psychological isolation, an inevitable uprooting, and the misconception that their home language and culture are to blame for lack of opportunity and equity they experienced in this country.

In working with Chicano students and families I have encountered some degree of transitionality in many, serious scars in some, and deeply seated resentment in a few. Does this mean that complete and forced assimilation does not work? Or that resistance to the integration of cultural values is preferable to forced assimilation? Richard Rodriguez *Hunger of Memory* (1982) is a classic example of the forced assimilation syndrome that has taken some Chicanos to the extreme of viewing their home language and culture as a barrier to success.

The price we have to pay for the neglect of immigrant children's language and culture as the means to succeed in our schools and to function well in other public institutions seems too high when we look at the social consequences of isolation, disenfranchisement, talent wasted and extended transitionality. As it was pointed out by the Spindlers in the chapter dealing with Menominee compensatory adaptation and transitionality, there is a high risk involved in attempts to cope with severely disjunctive culture change. The costs in psychological well-being and overall personality integration may be great. The sad consequences of extended transitionality and unsuccessful adjustment to mainstream society and its cultural values are evidenced in the overrepresentation of Chicanos in special education classes, correctional schools, jails, cult groups, drug and gang organizations, prostitution rings, and mental hospitals.

References

ACUNA, R. (1981) *Occupied America : A History of Chicanos*, 2d ed., New York, Harper and Row.

DELGADO-GAITAN, C. (1986) 'Teacher attitudes on diversity affecting student socio-academic responses: An ethnographic view', *Journal of Adolescent Research*, 1, pp. 1103–14.

DELGADO-GAITAN, C. (1987a) 'Traditions and transitions in the learning process of Mexican children: An ethnographic view', in G. SPINDLER AND L. SPINDLER (Eds) *Interpretive Ethnography of Education: At Home and Abroad*, Hillsdale, NJ, Laurence Erlbaum Associates, Publishers, pp. 333–59.

DELGADO-GAITAN, C. (1987b) 'Parent Perceptions of School: Supportive Environments for Children'. In H. TRUEBA (Ed.) *Success or Failure?: Learning and the Language Minority Student*, Cambridge, Newbury House Publishers, pp. 131–55.

McCARTHY K.F., and BURCIAGA VALDEZ, R. (1985) *Current and Future Effects of Mexican Immigration in California: Executive Summary*, The Rand Corporation Series: R–3365/1–CR, Santa Monica, CA, Rand Corporation.

McCARTHY, K.F., and BURCIAGA VALDEZ, R. (1986) *Current and Future Effects of Mexican Immigration in California*. The Rand Corporation Series: R–3365–CR, Santa Monica, CA, Rand Corporation.

ORNSTEIN, J. (Ed.) (1984) *Form and Function in Chicano English*. Rowly, MA, Newbury House.

RODRIGUEZ, R. (1982) *Hunger of Memory: The Education of Richard Rodriguez*, N.Y., Bantam Books.

RUEDA, R., and MEHAN, H. (1986) 'Metacognition and passing: Strategic interaction in the lives of students with learning disabilities'. *Anthropology and Education Quarterly*, 17, 3 139–65.

RUEDA, R. (1987) 'Social and communicative aspects of language proficiency in low-achieving language minority students'. in H. TRUEBA (Ed.) *Success or Failure: Linguistic Minority Children at Home and in School*, NY, Harper and Row, pp. 185–97.

SAN MIGUEL Jr., G. (1982) 'Mexican American organization and the changing politics of school desegregation in Texas, 1945–1980'. *Social Science Quarterly*, 13, pp. 701–715.

SAN MIGUEL Jr., G. (1986) 'One country, one language: An historical sketch of English language movements in the United States'. Paper commissioned by the Tomas Rivera Center. Claremont, CA.

SAN MIGUEL Jr., G. (1987) *Let all of them take heed*: Mexican Americans and the Campaign for Educational Equality in Texas, 1910–1981. Austin, TX, University of Texas Press.

SPINDLER, G. (1977) 'Change and continuity in American core cultural values: An anthropological perspective', in. G.D. DeRenzo (Ed.) *We the People*: *American Character and Social Change*, Westport, Greenwood, pp. 20–40.

SPINDLER, G. (1987a) 'Why have minority groups in North America been disadvantaged by their schools?', in G. SPINDLER (Ed.) *Education and Cultural Process: Anthropological Approaches, Second Edition*, Prospect Heights, Illinois, Waveland Press, Inc, pp. 160–172.

SPINDLER G. (1987b) 'The transmission of culture'. In G. SPINDLER (ed.) *Education and Cultural Process: Anthropological Approaches, Second Edition*, Prospect Heights, Illinois, Waveland Press, Inc, pp. 303–34.

SPINDLER, G., and SPINDLER, L. (1983) 'Anthropologists' view of American culture'. *Annual Review of Anthropology*, 12, pp. 49–78.

SPINDLER, G., and SPINDLER, L. (1987) *The Interpretive Ethnography of Education*: *At Home and Abroad*, Hillsdale, NJ, Lawrence Erlbaum Associates.

SUAREZ-OROZCO, M.M. (1989) *Central American Refugees and U.S. High Schools: A Psychosocial Study of Motivation and Achievement*, Stanford, CA, Stanford University Press.

TRUEBA, H. (1988a) 'Culturally-based explanations of minority students' academic achievement', *Anthropology and Education Quarterly*, 19, 3, pp. 270–87.

TRUEBA, H. (1988b). 'English literacy acquisition: From cultural trauma to learning disabilities in minority students', *Journal of Linguistics and Education*, 1, pp. 125–52.

TRUEBA, H. (1989) *Raising Silent Voices*: *Educating the Linguistic Minorities for the 21st Century*, New York, Harper and Row.

US DEPARTMENT OF COMMERCE (1987). 'The Hispanic Population in the United States: March 1986 and 1987 (Advance Report)', Washington, D.C., Government Printing Office.

VELEZ-IBANEZ, C. and MOLL, L. (1989) 'Funds of Knowledge: Networking in a Mexican Community of Tucson'. Research Report at the American Educational Research Association Meetings, San Francisco, 25–29 March.

Chapter 10

The Afro-American in the
Cultural Dialogue of the United States

Melvin D. Williams

The Black experience is an integral part of the American cultural dialogue, and that dialogue is molded and configurated by the continuing participation of the Afro-American. Indeed, one of the major differences between the American culture and the European culture is the influence of the Black experience. The cultural dialogue about such things as individual achievement and community, equality, conformity and difference, honesty and expediency, and success and failure take much of their conceptual strength from the participation of the Afro-American in the cultural dialogue of the United States. This has been true since the inception of the nation. The Black experience continues and will continue to play a major role in the American cultural dialogue.

As shown in Chapter 2, the twenty-first century will be one in which Caucasians are projected to become a minority in the United States, and the Black experience is the one that has exposed most Americans to human diversity (*Ebony*, 1989). The coming century will also be the one in which the world will become a global society, and again it is the Black experience that has socialized most Americans to cultural diversity.

The Black experience has stylistic impact on such things as hairstyles, teen concerts, music paraphernalia, music behavior, dance, fashions, language, rebellion, as well as changing basic values, such as the moral conscience of the US. The Black contribution to the American cultural dialogue is so intertwined and fundamental, that we can examine the Afro-American contribution by focusing on the cultural dialogue of the United States.

The Black experience itself is on trial today in the United States. The inner-city 'Grapes of Wrath' are testing the sinews of the most fundamental Black institution, the church. The Black church is one of the most important culture-transmitting and culture-sustaining institutions of the Black community. I have selected one Black church, Zion, in this chapter to demonstrate the problems and the solutions.

The Historical Context

It was the Afro-American experience that kept the ideals of the American Revolution close-at-hand and deep-in-heart. Freedom, liberty, opportunity, and individualistic pursuit of happiness were made real and poignant by the presence and the circumstances of the Black slave. Industrial capitalism, free enterprise, and the access to cheap labor were major components in the cultural dialogue of emancipation. As the United States turned to industrial and frontier expansion it created its vision of 'greatness' in part by the contrast to the insignificance of Blacks in America, and their exploitation and annihilation during Reconstruction and after, especially in the South. The First World War reminded the nation again of its ideals as Afro-Americans moved North and worked and created communities in Northern cities. Many Blacks were so deceived by this changing cultural dialogue that they created cultural and political movements (i.e., the 'Harlem Renaissance' and the Universal Negro Improvement Association) in response to the resurgence of American ideals. But the Great Depression brought them back to 'America's' earth, and once again Afro-America showed the United States the face of poverty, and helped to create the New Deal with its social legislation. The Black experience helped to create the myths of Franklin and Eleanor Roosevelt, and it challenged the spirit, visions and aspirations of Lyndon Johnson. Afro-Americans created a new social consciousness in the United States that infected the Kennedy family and many other Americans including Hubert Horatio Humphrey, the Freedom Riders, and Jimmy Carter. As I wrote in 1981 (1981b),

> Never forget the power of Black solidarity. Early in this century and late in the nineteenth century, it gave impetus to the labor movement. In the sixties, it infected White youth and they used our techniques to make ugly in, dirty cool, poor preferred, and war unacceptable. It set the stage for the women's movement, the concern for the aged, ethnic identity, and even gay liberation. Students in Paris and Peace People in Northern Ireland are singing 'We Shall Overcome Some Day'. Yes, Black became beautiful in the sixties, but we have started to relax and we cannot afford that kind of leisure.

Today it is the Black experience that creates and sustains the rhetoric pathos of the neo-conservatives in the United States. For these conservatives, Blacks should not have any compensation for historic denials, and the 'liberals' who support such compensation and any other such social welfare for Afro-Americans must be banned to political Siberia. Freedom must be confined to the opportunity to amass fortunes at the expense of labor, national resources, minorities, and women.

A Conceptual Framework

For twenty years my White students have informed me that their perceptions and attitudes towards poverty in America could not be sustained without the images they continually observe from the Afro-American experience. The images and the cultural dialogue of those Black experiences drive many Americans toward success and a level of achievement that is often irrational. Such images may not elicit a conscious response but derive their impact from the inferiority complex (after Alfred Adler, 1870–1937, Austrian psychiatrist and founder of individual psychology) that plagues most humans. The sight of poverty and its wretchedness reassures those more fortunate that they are not as 'inferior' as it simultaneously drives them to further demonstrate their 'superiority' by means of acquisitiveness. The inferiority complex cannot be assuaged. What kind of human requires millions of dollars, several large under-utilized houses and apartments, idle boats, cars, golf carts, and under-used jewelry and clothes to live a meaningful life? What kind of people accept such propaganda that this level of greed is necessary to fuel an economic system? And what sort of cultural dialogue validates this distribution of national resources in the face of the poor, the malnourished, the homeless, and the ever struggling middle-class? One answer to all of these questions is that these are people who are constantly exposed to images of the Black experience in America. Such images are interpreted by the values of the cultural dialogue and those interpretations validate it all. Who informs us that we can have a meaningful life without excess wealth? Who shows us that we can be denied status, wealth, power, fame, and material resources and yet enjoy our short time on earth with family and God? Of course, the Afro-American does among other disadvantaged groups.

One of the most important contributions of Afro-Americans to the American cultural dialogue, has been as a source of scholarly study which allows us to avoid focusing on the real social problems in the United States. We as social scientists understand the people in power (for example, the 'power elite' of Mills, 1956) that establish the designs for the cultural dialogue even within scholarship. Thus, we rarely study the irrational quest for status, wealth, power, fame and material possessions as a basis for our social problems. Instead we study the poor, and the Afro-American because they are different, accessible, and powerless.

As Hylan Lewis (1971:358) stated almost twenty years ago:

> My own view is that the most important research in this area now should focus not on the culture of poverty but on the culture of affluence — the culture that matters more and that is far more dangerous than the culture of poverty. Jean Mayer has put the thrust and the focus succinctly:

> There is a strong case to be made for a stringent population policy on exactly the reverse of the basis Malthus expounded. Malthus was concerned with the steadily more widespread poverty that indefinite population growth would invariably create. I am concerned about the areas of the globe where people are rapidly becoming richer. For rich people occupy much more space, consume more of each national resource, disturb the ecology more, and create more land, air, water, chemical, thermal and radioactive pollution than poor people. So it can be argued that from many viewpoints it is even more urgent to control the numbers of the rich than it is to control the numbers of the poor. (Mayer, 1969, p. 5)

As for diversity, the scientific community knows that race is a fictive and arbitrary category. All humans can mate and reproduce. They are one species. But the values and the cultural dialogue in America require a mythological separation of populations and groups for religious, regional, class, political, and ideological diversity and conflict. We utilize the conflict to reinforce American values and we will keep the diversity. But the diversity is only a part of the cultural dialogue. That part of the dialogue can be changed and it is changing. It will be better when race is no longer a dimension of it.

I am different from my mother, my siblings, my children, and my father, but I love all of them, and I include them in my family. American, German, and Japanese businesses have their differences (sometimes to our dismay) but they respect one another as members of the family of international enterprise. Any group or population that is arbitrarily separated is different. The cultural dialogue, however, determines the meaning of that difference. It can be a difference of inclusion or exclusion, and of fission or fusion. The Black experience helps to create the cultural dialogue about the American dream, but by design excludes most Afro-Americans from being included in its rewards. Martin Luther King had a different dream for a new cultural dialogue in the United States, and we must incorporate that dream if the cultural dialogue is to continue. People, groups, and populations are different, but the meaning of those differences are determined by the cultural dialogue. The value placed on the diversity can be made equal in the cultural dialogue. Only then can difference cease to be destructive.

Education

The Afro-American experience, as others, must be passed from generation to generation, and here the public school system has its role. As shown by the Spindlers in Chapter 5, the system as it now stands is designed to transmit middle class ideals and tools to the next generation. But the Black experience has sieged the public school system in most predominantly Black cities. Increasingly in the past score of years, the public school system and the inner cities have been abandoned for the suburbs by the middle class, both Black and White. The public school system in these cities now transmits mostly the Black experience to the next generation, and that experience is not fully accepted in the mainstream world of work and upward mobility (Williams, 1981a, 1989). Furthermore, many students have decided that it is not necessary to attend school to acquire this knowledge. The cultural dialogue must develop to the point where it includes the Black and other minority experiences in all aspects of its conversations. The recent trends have been for middle class Blacks and Whites to give poor Blacks their own turf, bereft of recognition, respect, and resources. This kind of isolation creates violence (gangs, crime against the person and property) and destruction (accelerated obsolescence). Those who flee to the suburbs mistakenly believe, that by physical separation, they can create different values, ideologies, and expectations. But the Blacks who live in the city are a part of the American cultural dialogue. They expect similar rewards from life and work as those in the suburbs and they will not be permanently denied by special separations. I present some examples from my research below.

Duane was bright, handsome and active. His mother had abandoned him and his aunt, a prostitution madam, reared him. Duane never wanted for anything. He had one of the few new cars in his ghetto neighborhood and the only one owned by a teenager. He had learned early from his aunt that wine, women and song were the good life. He loved fast horses, fine women, and good liquor, but he also excelled in his school work. His grades were B or above. He could have done better but he chose to 'hang out' with middle class teenagers who did not live in his neighborhood, but who welcomed him to theirs because of his money, looks, and car. Duane graduated from high school and his aunt sent him to law school. He completed his study and became a mediocre lawyer who spent most of his career in minor government jobs. Duane had chosen not to abandon his former way of life for the middle class lifestyles of others. He tried to integrate both lifestyles and he succeeded, but not as well in either as he might have.

Goodman was an intelligent, ambitious and active teen. His father had abandoned him, and his mother did domestic work to support them. His grandmother (while alive) attended him, but he was his own guardian most of the time while his mother was at work. His mother tried to provide well for him and his needs, and she succeeded. But Goodman wanted more, so he took jobs after school and sold newspapers, trying to sell more than any other newsboy. He outsold all but one. Goodman continued to be competitive all of his life, but he had no role models or encouragement to direct his energies and abilities toward education. On the contrary, he was encouraged to be a 'man', to have his own money, and to provide for his aging mother as she had provided for him. So he reluctantly completed high school and never considered college. Goodman worked hard at a variety of jobs until he discovered that the sale of drugs could earn him more income. He then pursued that enterprise and was successful for years. Eventually he was arrested, incarcerated and served his time. Today he again works hard as a city employee operating heavy equipment, but had he been advised and guided properly, he could have been a successful businessman or other professional.

Bullman was an abandoned child raised in a series of foster homes. He was bright, attractive and ambitious. After high school he enlisted in the US Army and rose to the rank of sergeant. When he returned home he used his Army benefits to attend a local university. He also used his Army service for hiring preference at the US Postal Service. He worked, attended classes, dressed well, rented a room (with use of the house) in a fashionable part of the city, and told whomever would listen that one day he would be the head of a major corporation. Of course, no one believed him and his friends doubted that he believed it. It seemed a part of his macho personality. He completed his studies in accounting and became a certified public accountant. When Bullman's long time sweetheart refused to marry him because of his bad temper and periodic drinking bouts, he packed up and moved to Los Angeles to seek his business fortune. For seven years he attempted to climb the corporate ladder, quitting positions that seemed dead end or that were 'too slow' in upward mobility. He had no comprehension of his limits and blamed all his failures on others. He soon acquired a reputation for wanting to be on the 'fast track' without the necessary ambition. He refused to accept the limitations and obstacles in corporate America for Blacks. Frustrated, he began to drink heavily, became downwardly mobile, and eventually he had a mental collapse. He returned to his hometown a broken man and he died in a mental institution.

Bullman's expectations were too high for his abilities and his circumstances. He could not accept any position that would not lead him to the 'top'. He refused to recognize that the little 'room at the top' might be too small for a Black, born poor in America. He could have had a good life if he had accepted some of his 'good' corporate positions, but he had to have it all.

Intense ambition must be tempered with the realization that age, ability, and opportunity will ultimately determine one's career level. Young students must be encouraged to be 'all that they can be,' but they must also be aware that somewhere, sometime, they may reach their career plateau. The greater the ambition and ability, the greater are the chances for success. But success, as most things in life, has its limits. And for those with such ability and ambition, those limits are difficult to endure. Bullman gave his life to his career, and never married or had children. While he could not accept his career limitations, he had a very close 'buddy' who had a parallel life. He watched helplessly as Bullman destroyed himself. He too reached his maximum level in accounting and he, though disillusioned, accepted it painfully. His response was to lower his expectations, enjoy his life with his children and to adjust some of his dreams.

Rodney was a bright teenager in his school, but he chose to 'get by' and he did only as much school work as necessary to pass from one grade to the next. He was large for his age and very handsome. He was popular with both girls and boys and he was respected because of his size and fighting ability. Many of the teenagers said Rodney was 'bad'. Rodney wanted 'big money fast' so he started to 'hustle the streets' even while finishing high school. He became involved in selling drugs, and at twenty he shot and killed a customer over a drug money dispute. He went to prison and, because he was large and 'a killer', he was respected there. He used his time in prison to earn a college degree and to write legal appeals. He became a 'jailhouse lawyer'. As a result of his legal writs he was released from prison after serving only five years. Once back on the streets he returned to crime. He robbed a bank and was sent back to prison. There he began another series of legal appeals until released four years later. He was finally incriminated in a murder-for-hire scheme and today faces execution.

Here was a brilliant mind that was not redirected into a career pattern. Rodney chose to do those things that he had learned early, and not to develop a new career path. Perhaps, had someone been able to influence him and redirect his energies and abilities, he would have become a great lawyer or some other professional, but no one reached Rodney in time.

The public school system too, will not escape judgment. As has been previously pointed out, the century will be one of great population diversity. The next century will also witness horse power replaced by brain power. And last but not least, the twentieth-first century will be one in which the world becomes a global society. Consequently no action in one nation will be separate from those in others. For all of these reasons the schools must prepare their students to understand and respect other cultures. My discussion on these pages clearly demonstrates that there must be significant changes if the schools specifically and the society generally is to transmit a cultural dialogue that will meet the requirements of the twentieth-first century.

The Community: Change, Diversity and Conflict

In one of the Black communities I have studied (Williams, 1984) there was once a viable commercial and residential neighborhood. The Black professionals and business people had an exclusive residential area, but it was located in the same neighbourhood where they applied their trades and practiced their professions. They were concerned about the entire neighborhood because it contained their offices and businesses, and their market.

On one street, the length of three city blocks, there was a florist, two medical doctors, five pharmacists, two funeral home directors, five shoe stores, a gasoline station, a music store, two variety stores, a hardware and lumber store, a meat market, two supermarkets, two paint stores, two beauty parlors, three professional photographer studios, a post office, a delicatessen, two movie theaters, a dance hall, a union hall for construction workers, a confectionery store, four clothing stores, two billiard parlors, a night club, an insurance office, an auto repair garage, and several grocery stores, restaurants and taverns. Most of the businesses were owned and operated by Afro-Americans. All of them at least had Black operators or employees. At the end of the business or professional day, most of the people went home in this same neighborhood. These people were proud of their schools, their churches, their Black politicians (i.e., constable, justice of the peace, ward chairman, and city councilman) and their 'four hundreds' (elite professionals and their families). The annual school picnic was a major holiday in this neighborhood, and the purchases from local merchants reached their peak for it. Every holiday had neighborhood celebrations and pageantry, and the neighbors' display of loyalty to their athletic teams. Many residents had no need or a desire to leave the neighborhood during their lifetime, as it was self contained. All the different social classes spent their days in each other's presence. Often poor children had a lower-middle class neighbor, who helped to socialize them, and every street had residents who were trying to 'uplift' the neighborhood. Children respected these residents and were embarrassed if caught by them engaging in inappropriate behavior. People were proud of where they lived, both the professional and the poor.

During the 1960s and the 1970s the enforcement of open housing laws and the prosecution of real estate interests that practiced segregation allowed Afro-Americans to buy and live in exclusive white neighborhoods. Racial stigmas began to ease and professional Blacks began to serve white clientele in formerly all white neighborhoods. The cultural dialogue sanctioned all of this as it represented upward mobility, more prestige, and validation of success. Many former residents of Black neighborhoods now boasted of residing on a street in which they were the only black family; of sending their children to a school in which only five Blacks were enrolled; or of having an all-white professional practice.

Meanwhile as a result of this outward migration the black neighborhood began to lose its middle-class residents and businesses, and professional people. Former storerooms and offices were occupied by pool rooms, 'jitney' stations, poorly stocked grocery stores run by inexperienced business operators, and by vending machines. The former orderliness of the street gradually disappeared as poorer Blacks took control of the street and the businesses. This decline forced the remaining middle class to move their enterprises.

In the residential areas the new black landlords divided the one family homes into several units in order to pay their mortgages and earn a profit. This high density of occupation changed these residential atmospheres and forced out the remaining middle class. Today, nothing remains of the commercial street area that I described earlier, and little reminiscent of the neighborhood at large. I witnessed the death of a neighborhood, and a way of life.

The cultural dialogue that created some cooperation between Whites and Blacks also established some basis for the conflict between Blacks of different classes. Blacks with the economic resources, the socialization, and the opportunity will conform to the mainstream models of behavior regardless of the costs to other Afro-Americans. Middle class Blacks often perceive themselves as different from lower and underclass Blacks, as do Whites.

The Role of the Church in the Black Experience

Zion is a Pentecostal church in Pittsburgh, Pennsylvania, whose ninety-one members intensively interact together in both religious and secular association. This church draws its members from several Black neighborhoods scattered throughout the city and must compete with other religious and secular groups for these members.

The members have restructured the mainstream values of American society into their own idiom. They have developed a communication code that serves constantly to create images of biblical stories and the traditional lifestyle in the rural South. The major themes of that code are food, animals, death, human anatomy, the physical world, and the supernatural. The code is all-inclusive. They have organized, conceptualized, and manipulated these themes into a distinctive ideology with which they determine their own identity and reduce the social distance generated by Zion's system of ranking.

This church is an aggregation of southern rural emigrants who settled in Pittsburgh and attempted to re-establish the nature of style of life they had known in the rural South. This required intensive solidarity among the members. In the urban context members were acutely aware of their limited access to the means of achieving power, position, recognition, money, and social mobility in the larger society, and recognized Zion as their alternative means for achieving these. This quest for mobility in Zion is the major basis for conflict in this church, and it is perceived as the greatest threat to the members' solidarity. Zion's response to the distinctive nature of its solidarity and its conflict is to: couch both solidarity and conflict within Zion's own symbol system, provide a variety of opportunities for intensive secular and sacred interaction, provide a wide range of membership tolerance which includes acceptance of those who are upwardly mobile and those who are hopelessly immobile, and to provide mechanisms of mobility and a system of ranking within Zion.

The church's activities use a great deal of the community's energies and resources. These sacred and secular activities provide the meaning and substance for the members' lives and absorb the competitive energies of its upwardly mobile members. The church organization also has its distinctive criteria for prestige and upward mobility, which are the bases for conflict in Zion, as members seek to maneuver within the system for higher status, to topple leadership for personal advantage, or to create schisms in the church in order to establish a new church and a different power structure within it.

The analysis of the nature of solidarity and conflict in Zion is critical to an understanding of this congregation. My analysis is primarily the result of participant observation, intensive interviewing, and the recording of life histories. The nature and quality of intensive interaction among these members creates a level of solidarity that should be characterized as community in the modern urban context. The nature of such communities upon the urban scene requires more attention for the proper analysis, description and understanding of modern society. The symbol subsystem, the instruments of mobility, the range of membership tolerance, and the nature of church activities in Zion give insight not only into the dynamics of Zion as a community, but also into the nature of black ethnicity in the context of modern urban society.

As a dynamic, interactional little community, Zion has been sustained not only by the ability to fulfill the needs of its original members but also by its ability to attract other poor Blacks whose temperament, character, capabilities, and life perspectives have been more suited to this church than to the other available subcultures in the Black ghetto of Pittsburgh. Most of the original members are deceased. In ten years most of those born in the rural South will have died. The competition of other ghetto subcultures will probably overwhelm Zion when the commitment of these southern members is no longer available. The mainstream society has changed in the last fifty years, and the avenues for Black achievement are not as restricted as they once were. Education is a growing value among Blacks and is becoming more and more available to them. The supportive ideology of Zion-salvation for the 'despised few' is becoming less and less meaningful in an aggressive and often militant age (*Black Scholar*, 1970). The purpose once served by Zion as a shelter for Black rural southern emigrants is becoming less and less important. The nature of urbanization itself will probably require very different human responses in the near future from those required in the recent past. Communities like Zion may no longer suffice for an isolated Black population facing new problems in an inner city and yet denied assimilation because of racist stigmata. But the commitment of service (see below) in Zion demonstrates for the Black middle class what it must do for the black inner cities.

The Church and the Black Middle Class

From slavery to 'freedom', from 'freedom' to 'economic exclusion', or 'from the plantation to the ghetto', the Black church has been crucial in the development of the Afro-American community and its leaders. Denied access to the wide range of institutional resources in America, the Black American has relied largely upon his or her church for the organizational training, socialization, social control, leadership development, and a sense of community. Such reliance and dependence has tended to 'overload' the churches in the black community. The Black church remains, today, a place where the poor and the economically successful should be able to come together in meaningful association and fellowship.

The relationship between the Black church and the Afro-American community continues to be essential for the sustenance and support of other

Black institutions, such as the family (Williams, 1986). However, the relationship between church and community has been significantly eroded as the Black middle class has achieved some access to mainstream life. As Lincoln (1984) observes in his recent review of black religion:

> The desegregation of schools, particularly at the college and university level, opened new doors of opportunity to Blacks. A veneer of desegregation in selected job markets meant new economic advancement for some, and created a small, highly visible black middle class increasingly conscious of its distance from which it was so recently rescued. The Black Church was directly affected by these events. It is little wonder, then, that there is paranoia in the Black Church, for the Black Church sees itself in the ominous shadow of conventional experience in integration. This is the crux of the matter, but that is not all.

Increasingly, the Black middle class does not live, serve, practice (professionally), or demand appropriate governmental services within the Black community. Middle-class Blacks often find themselves isolated in hostile White environments, and the poor Afro-Americans descend further into a hopeless underclass. Integration has been a double-edged sword. The perceptions of a declining significance of race (Wilson, 1978) in the minds of the Black middle class contributes to an abandoned underclass in inner cities, while the majority attitudes toward Afro-Americans of all classes is mainly determined by race and not by class.

That attitude of the Black middle class threatens the entire Black community, a community that cannot endure a racist multicultural society in which it is ignored by the majority and also abandoned by its own upwardly mobile members. The Black community and Black values are necessary for personal identity, growth, and development (Williams, 1973; 1975; 1978; 1980; 1982; and 1983). The Black church continues to be the stone upon which all these things must be built. These issues are examined and discussed below.

The withdrawal of the traditional church support of the Black family and the Black community is neither the result of the 'deradicalization' of the black church as Wilmore (1973) describes it for the first half of the twentieth century, nor the result of *Communitas* to status legitimation during the Great Depression as described by Mays and Nicholson (1969). On the contrary, it is a denial of allegiance to identity and its struggles. A willingness to abandon that allegiance to identity and social responsibility is, at present, the price for upward mobility within this society. That lack of support also contributes to the demise of vital institutions, (family, economic, education, etc.).

As DuBois (1963) told us, Blacks have two souls. To destroy one is to self-destruct. 'This double-consciousness, this sense of looking at oneself through the eyes of others, of measuring one's soul by the tape of a world that looks on in amused contempt and pity' (DuBois, 1963) cannot be assured except in personal fortitude and defiance. Black values, rooted in Black history, struggle, and contextual survival, are necessary for personal self-esteem and personal strength.

Community Service: The Zion Approach

The traditional Black church that brought Blacks from slavery to emancipation and from the Reconstruction and the 'Jim Crow' laws to the Civil Rights movement is being passively destroyed by the Black mainstream. The Black church and Black communities are being abandoned now by Black church members. The traditional ethic to serve in one's congregation and community is on the wane. Members come to church to display their clothes and coiffeurs rather than to build a church and community. Members participate in church and community to demonstrate their status and prestige rather than to enhance the quality of Black family life.

However, in Zion, a Pentecostal church with problems in its wider community similar to those of most inner cities, there were women and men who spent their lives trying to influence and direct the lives of the children and young adults of the congregation. The children thought that these adults were 'mean and ugly', but they respected them, often more than they respected their own parents; and they remembered them all of their lives as their fictive parents. This fictive extended family had the authority to scold and punish the children. These dedicated and committed women and men spent long hours, throughout many years, serving the congregation without tangible reward. They visited the sick and the elderly. They cooked and cleaned and prayed for them. They had group prayer meetings in the homes for those who desired it. When necessary they helped members move, managed their affairs, and provided them transportation. All these activities built the church and the community.

Yet these were only small examples of an abiding ethic to serve, that pervaded the congregation and benefited the young who were forced to attend church. This built the church and the community. This same ethic also socialized the children and set an example for the young adults. When one of these members received a periodic or final testimonial, it was 'much deserved' and often his or her only tangible reward. This philosophy of service is still true. The Zion Church continues to thrive.

It was in these social contexts that young people learned to value service, commitment, dedication, discipline, responsibility, Black identity and work, not wealth, status, prestige, recognition, and power as ends in themselves. For poor neighborhoods, destined to be poor, such values and attitudes are invaluable. These people did not have much money but they invested social capital in their children and young adults. Most members of Zion (Williams, 1974) did not desire 'to gain the whole world and lose their own souls.' That soul merged in their identity with their congregation and their commmunity, and they served it well.

Some people become rich and 'successful' by stealing, selling drugs, stolen goods, sex and pornography, but you cannot build good communities that way. The difference between the quest for individual and community wealth, status and power must be distinguished; waiting for the entire social system to change is pointless when Afro-American people are being destroyed now. The adult members of Zion guarded and directed their young as their future church. That is how they built a church and a community. It required a generation of character building, with close attention to child training. I did not understand that when I studied Zion; and I predicted (1974) that the church would disappear when all the elderly members were dead. I was wrong. I believed that social forces in the wider community would make the cohesive church group obsolete. It seemed to me that competing attractions in a viable Black community would destroy it. But the Zion members socialize their young to serve, and the church lives on.

I called these Black people, like those from Zion who are willing to serve in their churches and in their communities, 'core members'. But regardless of what they are called, Black communities with strained and traumatized Black families cannot survive and grow without them. Patience and sometimes painful tolerance are needed to really listen to the needs of the children in Zion. And even then the church did not have the necessary resources to provide for many of their needs. It took a strong commitment to help the children to learn the roles and potentials within the church, the community, the society, and the world. If the social capital is invested in them, it may return the dividends of mature, emotionally healthy, and intellectually active adolescents.

Black Youth in the American Cultural Dialogue

At other times and places, many families have generated upward mobility for their children by social, financial, and self-sacrifice. The parents work day and night so that their children might have the resources necessary for an education or their own businesses. Yet, these parents find the time to engage, challenge, and encourage their children to grow and develop. These parents have few ambitions for themselves and obtain their greatest pleasures from the small successes of their children. These social and self investments allow the next generation to move substantially ahead, and they instill in that generation the models and roles for another cycle of upward mobility. Some families do not have the parents capable of achieving this alone. Other families have so many children that notwithstanding their efforts, they do not have the social, emotional, or energy capital. But if they have their church, their kin, and their community with people who are there to serve, the same goals are accomplished.

Working parents, single-parent households, isolated nuclear families, individualism, and the demise of the traditional Black church and Black community are playing havoc with the growth and development of Black youth in America. These adversities are the results of materialism, inflation, unemployment, and urbanization in the larger society. Parents must deny themselves the new car, the club membership, the expensive sport, the parties, a new house, and clothing in order that the children will get more social and material capital. Afro-Americans must decide between loyalty to youth, development of community, faith, trust, commitment in the Black church and community, or selfish, large, wealthy, socially prominent congregations. Middle-class status and mainstream lifestyles must not replace the traditional social responsibility of the Black church. A cosmetic commitment is not enough. We need 'core members' like those who served in Zion (Williams, 1983).

Let me briefly state a few benefits of core members to the youth in that church. Pregnancy, often sex itself, was not tolerated before marriage. It was a serious sin with severe social sanctions and members were ostracized if discovered. Children competed in Sunday school classes, and young adults and teenagers competed both there and in Sunday evening classes. They showed their 'stuff' on knowing and understanding the Bible and the meanings of the Bible stories. Teenagers and young adults vied for acting parts in the Christmas and Easter church plays, and then, when successful, tried to out-perform one another. Teenagers competed for church positions such as announcer, junior ushers, junior choir members, junior chorus members and the 'lead' singers. Pre-teens and teenagers served in the church kitchen and dining halls as busboys and busgirls, as dishwashers, waiters, waitresses, cashiers, and errand people. The only rewards for these jobs were praise, the appreciation of the adults, the opportunity to be seen and be well-fed. Thus, the youth in Zion not only learned to work, but they also learned how to value and protect their positions.

Zion Church was created because the Black mainstream did not want its members to worship in their churches. In the classic mainstream style the individualism of self and nuclear family may become the new creed: 'All I need from the church is status, prestige, and recognition, so all I give is money.'

As much as the historical 'pie in the sky' Black church tradition (as a survival technique) may deserve its criticism, the Black church remains the primary Black institution in America. My own bias here reflects a sense of urgency. I know that the Zion Church represents an extreme in religious behavior, but the behavior I have seen elsewhere appears to be a bipolar opposite. Neither is the ideal. Zion has some features and themes that seem appropriate for the 1990s.

The faltering middle-class church is not the result of a changing orientation in black church life from *Gemeinschaft* to *Gesellschaft* (Mukenge, 1983). It is the result of failing Black commitments and responsibilities in a White controlled society. Failure that Blacks can no longer endure, especially, in the inner cities of America.

The Black church, that central institution in the Black community since slavery, is being challenged today with major social problems. Black youth are high school drop-outs, teenage mothers, jail residents, unemployed — unemployable — victims of crime, drug abusers, college dropouts, and members of the economic underclass in alarming numbers. All of this is occurring at a time when there is an eclipse of commitment to the poor and disadvantaged from governmental units and from American society in general.

These mounting social problems are a potential dilemma for the Black church. Once again the church may be called upon to care for the Black poor and disadvantaged. Regardless of the causes, the status of Afro-America is not good and this is the present challenge of the Black church in the American cultural dialogue.

No one denies the significance of the Black church as a focal institution among Afro-Americans, yet little research has been conducted to determine how the Black church can continue to be effective in comtemporary America. Church and community both require social investments of time, energy and emotional capital. One answer is to persuade and convince the people to serve in their church and to serve and live in their own community.

Mainstream Blacks can learn from history. If poor Black masses are ignored and abandoned, then you must deal with those Black leaders who take up the clarion call of the Black underclass — Booker T. Washington, Marcus Garvey, H. Rap Brown, Malcolm X, Huey Newton, Bobby Seale, heretical preachers, Jim Jones, Daddy Grace, Father Devine and Rev. Ike, etc.

The Black mainstream church members are learning their lessons well from their white role models. It is reminiscent of the corporate executives who routinely chair with great fanfare community charity projects as cosmetic adjuncts to their corporate careers. They seldom, if ever, have the time or the commitments to devote their energies to any of the unheralded tasks that every community requires. But the Black church and the Black community cannot afford such elitism as both are only a mere 120 years out of slavery. The Black church and the Black community, deprived of *esprit de corps* and commitment in these ways that I have described, doom most Blacks to a desperate underclass with all the social problems that most of us know so well. Blacks can invest their social capital in their church, their people, and their community or watch the whole enterprise go socially bankrupt. That process has already begun. Now is the time for unselfish investments in Black youth.

Conclusion

The structure of power in this society manipulates all of us to its own ends. Thus, we all share some of the blame for social problems. But apportioning blame is not the goal here, but rather the suggesting of resolutions to some of the predicaments. As a student of human behavior I know well that social problems and their solutions are never simple. I do not mean to suggest that here. But I am attempting to strongly suggest that the ethos of service and commitment to the Black church and the Black community is one of the most important places to begin to resolve some of the predicaments that I have discussed here.

If the present trends continue, we may not only have to bus our children for a 'quality' education but also for worship. The Black middle class may remember how integration is won and continue to pay their own dues. Like the students of Africa educated abroad, they may return home to the Black community. They may continue to make the social and political demands that may save these communities and those that reside in them. That may not be done effectively unless they live there. Then the Black community may become an acceptable place for all Afro-Americans to live and particularly for Black children to grow and develop. The upwardly mobile Black may not only be economically successful but also may be socially responsible, for the quest for strong congregations and communities will elude them as long as the ethic of service does.

Finally, we must acknowledge the classic dilemmas in the conflict of class. The antagonisms between those who are upwardly mobile and their downwardly mobile Black brothers and sisters are also a part of the cultural dialogue. It is the stuff, essence, and motivation of achievement and success in this society. It is rooted in the human dialogue and we must change the human language if the human animal is to avoid the fate of the dinosaur.

References

Black Scholar (1970) 'The Black Church', *Black Scholar*, **2**, no.4, pp. 3–49.

DuBois, W.E.B. (1963) *The Souls of Black Folk*, New York, Harper Torchbooks.

Ebony (1989) 'The Biggest Secret of Race Relations: The New White Minority' *Ebony* **44**, p. 84.

Lewis, H. (1971) 'Culture of Poverty? What does it matter,' in *The Culture of Poverty: A Critique*, E.B. Leacock, (Ed.), New York, Touchstone pp. 345–63.

Lincoln C.E. (1984) *Race, Religion and the Continuing American Dilemma*, New York, Hill and Wang.

Mays, B.E. and Nicholson J.W. (1969) *The Negroes' Church*, New York, Russell and Russell.

Mills, C.W. (1956) *The Power Elite*, New York, Oxford University Press.

Mukenge, I.R. (1983) *The Black Church in Urban America*, Lanham, MD, University Press of America.

Williams, M.D. (1973a) 'The Black Community,' Special Hillman Issue, *The Pastoral Institute Newletter*, **1**, p. 12.

Williams, M.D. (1973b) 'Food and Animals: Behavior Metaphors in a Black Pentecostal Church in Pittsburgh' *Urban Anthropology* **2**, p. 74.

Williams, M.D. (1974) *Community in a Black Pentecostal Church: An Anthropological Study*, Pittsburgh, University of Pittsburgh Press.

Williams, M.D. (1975a) 'Social Cohesion in a Low Income Black Neighborhood in Pittsburgh,' in *Selected Readings in Afro-American Anthropology*, M.D. Williams (Ed.) Lexington, Xerox Publishing Company.

Williams, M.D. (1975b) *Selected Readings in Afro-American Anthropology*, Lexington, Xerox Publishing Company.

Williams, M.D. (1978) 'Childhood in an Urban Black Ghetto: Two Life Histories' *UMOJA* (University of Colorado at Boulder) **2**, pp. 169–182.

Williams, M.D. (1980) 'Belmar: Diverse Life Styles in a Pittsburgh Black Neighborhood,' *Ethnic Groups: An International Journal of Ethnic Studies*, **3**, pp. 23–54.

Williams, M.D. (1981a) 'Observations in Pittsburgh Ghetto Schools,' *Anthropology and Education Quarterly*, **12** (Fall), pp. 211–220.

Williams, M.D. (1981b) *On the Street Where I Lived*, New York, Holt, Rinehart, and Winston.

Williams, M.D. (1982) 'Used Car Domain: An Ethnographic Application of Clustering and Multidimensional Scaling' with J.M. Roberts and George Poole, in H.C. Hudson, (Ed.), *Classifying Social Data: New Applications of Analytic Methods for Social Science Research*, San Francisco, Jossey Bass.

Williams, M.D. (1983a) 'Notes From a Black Ghetto in Pittsburgh,' *Critical Perspective of Third World America: Race, Class, Culture in America*, Berkeley, California, **1**, pp. 196–208.

Williams, M.D. (1983b) 'The Conflict of Corporate Church and Spiritual Community: An Ethnographic Analysis' in C.S. Dudley (Ed.), *Building Effective Ministry: Theory and Practice in the Local Church*, New York, Harper and Row, pp. 55–67.

WILLIAMS, M.D. (1984) *Community in a Black Pentecostal Church: An Anthropological Study*, paper edition, Prospect Heights, Illinois, Waveland Press.

WILLIAMS, M.D. (1986) 'Examining the Community Through their Congregations: Ethnography in a Small Midwestern City,' *The Griot*, 5, pp. 13–21.

WILLIAMS, M.D. (1989) 'Education for the Disadvantaged Student', *The Griot*.

WILMORE, G.S. (1973) *Black Religion and Black Radicalism: An Examination of the Black Experience in Religion*, Garden City, NY, Doubleday.

WILSON, W.J. (1978) *The Declining Significance of Race: Blacks and Changing American Institutions*, Chicago, University of Chicago Press.

Chapter 11

Final Thoughts

George and Louise Spindler

These final thoughts were written immediately after another trip by car across the US from the West Coast to Wisconsin. We drove through the heartland, in a straight line eastward, more or less, through California, Nevada, Utah, Wyoming, South Dakota, Nebraska, Iowa and on a diagonal through Wisconsin: from Mississippian bluffs to the mixed conifers and softwood forests of the northeast. Once we left Salt Lake City behind us, we crossed the interstate freeways occasionally but rarely travelled on them. We didn't camp along the way as we have so many times, but stayed in motels, one a 'Ma and Pa' establishment we had stopped at before, another one owned and operated by a Pakistani family, and the rest were operated by motel chains that boast of their ability to provide all the necessities and some of the luxuries for the traveller at a modest cost. As one sign in the parking area of one of the motels said, 'When you are asleep, we look to you just like those fancy motels you would pay twice as much for'. They provided the necessities all right, and for many parts of the world they would be penultimate luxuries: soft, clean beds, functional bathrooms with ample hot water and clean towels, cable TV with free movies, and, oh yes, free coffee in the office and a swimming pool. We were reminded of the material richness in the USA, a richness that many Americans take for granted but some have little opportunity to enjoy.

We saw no obvious poverty anywhere. We have always avoided cities and this trip took us only through Salt Lake City on a newly redone interstate but otherwise through small towns and villages on state highways. We traversed hundreds of miles of open semi-desert and high prairie, and hundreds more through rich farmlands. Most of the terrain we traversed was, by European standards, scarcely occupied. We were reminded again of the geographic immensity of the United States, and of the low population density in non-metropolitan hinterland areas.

When we arrived at our destination, itself in the hinterland of northeast central Wisconsin near Roseville, we visited with people we know well, whom we count as friends (and they us). The talk was of forest, lake and stream, drought and rainfall, the price of land and its products, local events, other people, deaths, family, only a little about politics and not at all about international affairs. It was the same conversation that we had carried on now and then as we crossed the country and stopped to chat at filling stations, cafes, our motels for the night, and it was the same conversation we had heard on the local radio stations in the car as we cruised through their licensed wavelength areas.

When we turned on our television to catch the ten o'clock news, securely ensconced in our north woods home many miles from anything resembling a city, we heard parts of President Bush's declaration of war on drugs followed by interviews with police chiefs, politicians, and some established activists in the 'war on drugs'. We saw street scenes of drug transactions and emergency rooms in hospitals where victims of drug-related violence were received in numbers too great to permit effective treatment for all; we saw dozens of babies, born of mothers on crack, who will be learning-disabled if they live at all. All of the babies shown were Black. The street scenes were from predominantly Black East Oakland, California. Drug use in America, to be sure, is not a Black problem alone, although this was the impression given by the TV coverage we saw.

East Oakland is a part of America and its inhabitants are Americans and they are participants in the American dialogue. From where we viewed them in our secure hinterland niche they seemed far away. If we didn't know better and if we were not professionals concerned with equity for minorities we might easily dismiss the images and talk on the tube as irrelevant to our lives, hopes, ambitions, and even to our welfare. East Oakland and its drug problems, its violence, its poverty, and its apparent hopelessness seem like someone else's problem, and more foreign to us than the Indian reservations of northern Wisconsin. However, there is a drug problem and violence in these reservations and in the cities bordering Lake Michigan. Their problems are of the same kind as those of East Oakland, though of lesser magnitude, and they are located within less than a day's travel by car from our northwoods home. In the nearby small town of Arcadia and the larger Riverfront City, there are drugs and violence, but on such a diminished scale that they do not seem very important to those not involved.

The drug barons, the dealers, the street pushers and drug users are all participants in the American dialogue. The distributors and pushers are pursuing success. They are achieving. They are entrepreneurs. Some of them, like the descendants of the Mafia, will become 'respectable' mainstream citizens if they can accumulate enough wealth to retire and live the good life. The users of their sold product are participants in the dialogue for other, also related, reasons. They are taking out their disappointment, their anger, their feeling of being unfairly treated by fate and by society, their neglect by society, and their pervasive sense of relative deprivation, in their use of drugs. The users know what success looks like in America. They see it hour after hour on the television. They also see it in person in affluent Oakland and the greater Bay Area of California. Drug users in Oakland can watch stretch limousines roll by (but not in their neighborhood) and think about the way the people in them live. Drug and alcohol abuse, violence, child abuse, and sexual exploitation of children, are all forms of participation in the dialogue, a perversion of the search for success, created by inequity. It is hard to live in a society where the drive for material success is held up as the basic goal of life and where, ideally, anyone can achieve success if they try hard enough.

The enemy in America is not drugs but inequity. The disparity between the poisonous condition of the inner city and the affluence of the suburbs and high-rise apartments, between the mainstream rich and the minority poor, between Black and White, perverts the dialogue of achievement, success, hard work, honesty, individualism, optimism, independence, and equality. It is the enemy within that erodes and may destroy the dialogue. Drug use and its consequences are symptoms, not underlying causes. Our governing officials, however, and the programs they generate will not deal with the underlying causes. The overwhelming facts of inequity in America will be largely ignored in the self-deluded fantasy that drugs can be controlled by massive interdiction at our borders and beyond, and by police raids and jail sentences.

Inequity in America has been created by the dialogue of achievement, of individualistic striving for success, perverted into self-aggrandizement. The dialogue of equality, honesty, concern for others, is still alive but has lost ground to the opposition, the dialogue of extreme self interest, within the total complex of values and motivations. The underlying problem is not drugs, or violence, but individualistic, self-oriented success, the successful drive for wealth by individuals uncommitted to the public good.

But, one may object, young professional and business people use drugs (although in decreasing numbers) and they are not on the short end of inequity. They too suffer the pangs of a pervasive sense of relative deprivation. With both husband and wife working full time, they may achieve an income that should, if the 'dream' works, assure them of security and a measure of happiness, but it does not. They cannot have what their parents of the same socio-economic status had more easily. The honest rewards of honest achievement seem illusory to many. In a drug-oriented culture the promise of immediate relief for overindulgence and any ordinary ache or pain by simply taking any one of an array of over-the-counter drugs

— the use of drugs is a natural remedy for disappointment. The dialogue is out of balance. The drive for material success is obsessive. It produces inequity in the distribution of opportunity and disappointment on the part of the very ones supposed to be succeeding. For a little while in the 1960s and the early 1970s, the linkages between work, success and happiness, were challenged by the opposition who emphasized concern for others, the necessity of self-knowledge, and the search for happiness (a general state of satisfaction). But in the 1980s the drive for material success rather than spiritual has dominated. Perhaps the American dialogue is self correcting and we will achieve a better balance in the decades ahead. However, it is our conviction that unless we find the means to reduce inequity in economic and educational opportunities, and provide opportunities for productive, socially aware self expansion, our national cultural dialogue will become increasingly dysfunctional and become so distorted, so perverted, that continuity with our past will be seriously eroded, perhaps destroyed.

In the hinterland the obsessive drive for material success and the inequity it produces are not so obvious and people seem to retain self respect in spite of that inequity which does exist. This is a major difference between at least some of the hinterland and metropolitan America, that has not entered sufficiently into our analysis.

To be sure equity is not created from only the top down. Equity is achieved as well as legislated and managed. As scholars such as John Ogbu, Marcelo Suarez-Orosco, and Margaret Gibson have made clear by their researches on the new immigrants such as the Punjabis, refugees from Central America, Vietnamese, and others, America is still a land of opportunity for highly motivated individuals who believe in the system. Many persons among the new immigrant populations achieve academic and economic success despite enormous obstacles of language, cultural difference, and socio-economic disadvantage.

A trip through the heartland-hinterland is reassuring. The dialogue of equality and concern for friends and relatives is alive and well there; it is also troubling because the capacity for isolation from glaring discrepancies between our culturally and politically phrased ideals and the realities of life in America for millions of our citizens is so profound. This is a time in our history for awareness.

There are other considerations we might bring into a final comment. For example we have not made much of the probable decline of the influence and power of the referent ethniclass. That the position of this class is eroding as the American cultural process continues to absorb new populations and new cultural elements, and old, historically established boundaries break down, is not to be gainsaid. In the long run, however, this decline is not important to cultural continuity or social health. The

American cultural dialogue is a process that is not the product or possession of any particular class or ethnic group. The value orientations and their oppositions that constitute the mainstream version of the dialogue have been formed by history and that history defined White Anglo-Saxon, North European, Protestant culture as a primary cultural force in the development of American culture. These values are there for anyone to use, and they are being used.

We can expect to see increasing conflicts among ethnic groups and between ethnic groups and the 'non-ethnic' mainstream. Ethnic groups, particularly Blacks and Hispanics, will compete for their share of the benefits. Middle and upper class mainstream Americans will resent incursions into their socio-economic and cultural territory as the economy continues to express the uncertainties of the modern world, the continuing destruction of the environment, and the critical mass of the Third World. Members of the working class White mainstream will continue to defend their jobs, homes, and neighborhoods from penetration by people of color. Even, however, as these battles are being fought, the boundaries between 'ethnic' and 'non-ethnic' and between mainstream and minority will become more and more blurred. For many young people they have become quite irrelevant, as among the high school students described by Alan Peshkin in a West Coast school.

Through it all the American cultural dialogue will endure. Americans are attempting to do what no one else has done in the pursuit of liberty, justice and equal opportunity for all citizens. The dialogue is a process, not a fixed entity; there is continuity and there is change. Though in the 1980s, inequity in the distribution of power, wealth and opportunity in our society has been dramatic and destructive, there are forces working toward social and economic justice that are also embedded in the dialogue. We are hopefully heading into a new cycle in that dialogue, where the oppositions to inequity may become (at least temporarily) dominant.

Notes

Equity cannot be considered to be a sufficient 'single factor' cause of drug abuse. In Zurich, Switzerland, for example, there is a park set aside for drug abusers and free needles are supplied (Sixty Minutes, television program, January 18, 1990). Many of the abusers come from relatively well-off families. Drug abuse is difficult to explain under these circumstances. There are multiple causes. The equity issue appears to be relevant to a scene in the USA. Alan Peshkin (1991) describes a California high school in a multicultural environment that is characterized by strong cultural diversity.

Stereotypic prejudice is low or absent and racial/ethnic boundaries are weak. John Ogbu (1987) and Marcelo Suarez-Orosco (1989) analyze the 'new immigrants' and their struggle to participate in the American dialogue.

Appendix 1

Case Studies on Aspects of American Culture from *Case Studies in Cultural Anthropology* edited by George and Louise Spindler

APPLEBAUM, H. (1981) *Royal Blue: The Culture of Construction Workers.*

ASCHENBRENNER, J. (1975) *Lifelines: Black Families in Chicago*, (Reprinted by Waveland Press, 1983).

BASSO, K. (1970) *The Cibecue Apache.*

DANER, F. (1974) *The American Children of Krsna: A Study of the Hare Krsna Movement.*

DAVIDSON, R. (1974) *Chicano Prisoners: The Key to San Quentin.*

DOUGHERTY, M. (1978) *Becoming a Woman in Rural Black Culture.*

DOWNS, J. (1971) *The Navajo* (Reprinted by Waveland Press, 1984).

DOWNS, J. (1966) *The Two Worlds of the Washo.*

ESMAN, M. (1986) *Henderson, Louisana: A Cajun Community.*

FRIEDLAND and NELKIND (1971) *Migrant: Agricultural Workers in America's Northeast.*

GAMST, F. (1980) *Hoghead: An Industrial Ethnology of the Locomotive Engineer.*

GROBSMITH, E. (1981) *Lakota of the Rosebud: A Contemporary Ethnography.*

HICKS, G. (1976) *Appalachian Valley.*

HOEBEL, A. (1977) *The Cheyennes*, (2nd ed.)

HOSTETLER, J. and HUNTINGTON, G. (1980) *The Hutterites in North America* (Fieldwork Edition).

JACOBS, J. (1974) *Fun City: A Retirement Community* (Reprinted by Waveland Press, 1983).

KEHOE, A. (1989) *The Ghost Dance Religion: Ethnohistory and Revitalization.*

KEISER, L. (1979) *The Vicelords: Warriors of the Streets* (Fieldwork Edition).

KUNKEL, P. and KENNARD, S. (1971) *Spout Spring: A Black Community in the Ozarks.*

MCFEE, M. (1972) *Modern Blackfeet: Montanans on a Reservation* (Reprinted by Waveland, 1984).

MADSEN, W. (1974) *The Mexican-Americans of South Texas* (2nd ed.).

O'TOOLE, J. (1972) *Watts to Woodstock* (Los Angeles and South Africa).

PARTRIDGE, W. (1972) *Hippie Ghetto* (Gainesville) (Reprinted by Waveland Press, 1985).

PILCHER, W. (1972) *Portland Longshoremen*.

SPINDLER, G. and SPINDLER, L. (1971) *Dreamers with Power: The Menominee* (Reprinted by Waveland, 1984, with new Foreword).

SAFA, H. (1974) *The Urban Poor of Puerto Rico*.

SUGARMAN, B. (1974) *Daytop Village* (a drug therapy community).

WILLIAMS, M. (1981) *On the Street Where I Lived* (Black Pittsburgh Community).

WONG, B. (1982) *Chinatown in New York City*.

From *Case Studies in Education and Culture* edited by George and Louise Spindler

COLLIER, J. (1973) *Alaskan Eskimo Education*.

HOSTETLER, J. and HUNTINGTON (1990) *Children in Amish Society: Socialization and Community Education* (Revised edition).

ROSENFELD, J. (1971) *'Shut Those Thick Lips': Ethnography of a Slum School* (Reprinted by Waveland Press, 1983).

WARD, M. (1971) *Them Children: A Study in Language Learning* (Reprinted by Waveland Press, 1986).

WOLCOTT, H. (1973) *The Man in the Principal's Office: an Ethnography* (Reprinted by Waveland Press, 1984).

Case Studies in Cultural Anthropology, Fort Worth, Holt, Rinehart and Winston.

Case Studies in Education and Culture, Fort Worth, Holt, Rinehart and Winston.

Selected titles, as indicated, have been reprinted by Waveland Press, Prospect Heights, IL.

References

Chapters 1 through 8, and Chapter 11

The references below are cited in the End Notes, excepting for the following, included because they are relevant to the argument of the text but not specifically cited: Aschenbrenner, *American Anthropologist*, Bellah *et al.*, Davis, De Mause, Henry, Hsu, Jenkins, Lynd (1929 and 1937), Merelman, Moffat, Nash, Perin (1988), Schneider, Shortridge, Varenne (1977, 1986).

ANDERSON, CHARLES, (1970) *White Protestant Americans*, Englewood Cliffs, New Jersey, Prentice-Hall.

American Anthropologist (1955) 'The USA as Anthropologists see it', 57, pp. 1113–80. Special issue, LANTIS, M. (Ed.).

APPLEBAUM, HERBERT, A. (1981) *Royal Blue: The Culture of Construction Workers*, New York, Holt, Rinehart and Winston.

ASCHENBRENNER, JOYCE S. (1974) *Black Lifelines*, New York, Holt, Rinehart and Winston. (Reprinted by Waveland Press Prospect Heights, Ill. in 1987).

BELLAH, ROBERT, MADSEN, R., SULLIVAN, W., SWINDLER, A., and TIPTON, S. (1985) *Habits of the Heart: Individualism and Commitment in American Life*, Berkeley, University of California Press. (Published in paper edition by Harper and Row, New York, (1986), as a Perennial Library book).

BERRY, WENDELL, (1977) *The Unsettling of America: Culture and Agriculture*, New York, Avon.

BLOOM, ALLAN, (1987) *The Closing of the American Mind*, New York, Simon and Schuster.

CLINTON, CHARLES, (1973) 'The Social Organization of an Occupational Subsociety: An Ecological Approach to the Carpenters of Local 1281'. Ph.D. dissertation, Washington State University.

COLLIER, JANE (1974) 'Women in Politics', in M. ROSALDO, L. LAMPHERE, eds. *Women, Culture and Society*, Stanford, CA., Stanford University Press.

DE BEAUVOIR, S. (1953) *The Second Sex*, New York, Knopf.

DE CREVECOEUR, M.G. ST JEAN, 'This American, this New Man', from *Letters from an American Farmer*, in RAPSON, R. (Ed.) (1967) pp. 15–18 (see entry).

DE TOQUEVILLE, A. (1901) *Democracy in America,* trans. by H. REEVE, New York, Appleton, in RAPSON, R. (ed.) (1967) (see entry).

DANER, FRANCINE JEANNE, (1976) *The American Children of Krsna: A Study of the Hare Krsna Movement,* New York, Holt, Rinehart and Winston.

DAVIS, GLENN, (1976) *Childhood and History in America,* New York, Psycho-history Press.

DEMAUSE, LLOYD, (1984) *Reagan's America,* New York, Creative Roots, Inc.

DEVOS, G. (1980) 'Ethnic Adaptation and Minority Status', *Journal of Cross-Cultural Psychology.* **11**, 1, pp. 101–124.

ESMAN, MARJORIE, (1986) *Henderson, Louisiana: Cultural Adaptation in a Cajun Community,* New York, Holt, Rinehart and Winston.

FESTINGER, LEON *et al.* (1956) *When Prophecy Fails: A Social and Psychological Study of a Modern Group That Predicted the Destruction of the World,* New York, Harper and Row.

FUJITA, MARIKO and SANO, TOSHIYUKI, (1988) 'Children in American and Japanese Day Care Centers: Ethnography and Reflective Cross-Cultural Interviewing', in H. TRUEBA and C. DELGADO-GAITAN, (1988) *Education and Society: Learning Content through Culture,* New York, Praeger.

FUSSELL, PAUL, (1983) *Class: A Painfully Accurate Guide through the American Status System,* New York, Ballantine Books.

GIBSON, MARGARET, (1987) 'Punjabi Immigrants in an American High School', in *Interpretive Ethnography of Education at Home and Abroad,* G. and L. SPINDLER, (eds), Hillsdale, N.J., Lawrence Erlbaum.

GILLIN, J. (1955) 'National and regional cultural values in the United States', *Social Forces,* **34**, pp. 107–13.

GOLDMAN, SHELLEY and MCDERMOTT, R. (1987) 'The culture of competition in American Schools', in *Education and Cultural Process: Anthropological Approaches,* G. SPINDLER, (ed.), Prospect Heights, Ill., Waveland Press.

GORDON, M. (1964) *Assimilation in American Life.* Oxford University Press.

GORER, G. (1948) *The American People: A Study in American Character,* New York, Norton.

HALLOWELL, A. IRVING (1957) 'The Backwash of the Frontier: The Impact of the Indian on American culture', in *The Frontier in Perspective,* W. WYMAN, C. KROEBER (eds) Madison WI, University of Wisconsin Press, pp. 229–58.

HARRIS, MARVIN, (1986) *Why Nothing Works,* New York, Simon and Schuster, Inc.

HATCH, ELWIN, (1979) *Biography of a Small Town,* New York, Columbia University Press.

HENRY, JULES, (1963) *Culture Against Man,* New York, Random House.

HICKS, GEORGE, L. (1976) *Appalachian Valley,* New York, Holt, Rinehart and Winston.

HOSTETLER, JOHN and HUNTINGTON, GERTRUDE, (1976) *Children in Amish Society: Socialization and Community Education,* New York, Holt, Rinehart and Winston.

HOSTETLER, JOHN and HUNTINGTON, GERTRUDE, (1980) *The Hutterites in North America,* Fieldwork ed., New York, Holt, Rinehart and Winston.

VON HÜBNER, G. (1874) *A Ramble around the World*, 2 vols. London, Macmillan, in RAPSON, R. (ed.) (1967) pp. 22–25 (see entry).

HSU, FRANCIS, (1953). *Americans and Chinese: Two Ways of Life*. New York, Schuman.

HSU, FRANCIS L.K. (1981) *Americans and Chinese : Passage to Differences*, 3rd ed. Honolulu, The University Press of Hawaii.

JACOB, EVELYN and JORDAN, CATHIE (eds) (1987) *Anthropology and Education Quarterly*, **18**, 4. A theme issue 'Explaining the School Performance of Minority Students'.

JEFFERSON, THOMAS, (1781) 'The Moral Independence of the Cultivators of The Earth', in RAPSON, R. (Ed.) (1967) pp. 18–19 (see entry).

JENKINS, PETER and BARBARA, (1981) *The Walk West: A Walk Across America 2*, New York, Ballantine Books.

JOHNSON, NEIL H. (1975) *The Real People: A Rural New York Community*, Unpublished manuscript.

KLUCKHOHN, CLYDE, (1949) *Mirror for Man*. New York, McGraw-Hill.

KLUCKHOHN, CLYDE, (1951) 'Values and Value-Orientations', in *Toward a General Theory of Action*, T. PARSONS, E. SHILLS, (eds.), pp. 388–433. Cambridge, MA.

KLUCKHOHN, FLORENCE, (1950) 'Dominant and Substitute Profiles of cultural orientation', *Social Forces* **28**, pp. 376–93.

KUNKEL, PETER and KENNARD, SARA S. (1971) *Spout Spring: A Black Community*, New York, Holt, Rinehart and Winston.

LABARRE, WESTON, (1962) *They Shall Take Up Serpents: The Psychology of the Southern Snake Handling Cult*, Minneapolis, University of Minnesota Press.

LEAST HEAT MOON (TROGDOM, WILLIAM) (1982) *Blue Highways: A Journey into America*. New York, Fawcett Crest.

LIEBERMAN, STANLEY and WATERS, MARY, (1988) *From Many Strands: Ethnic and Racial Groups in Contemporary America*, N.Y. Russell Sage Foundation, in *ITEMS Social Science Research Council* 43, 1, (1989), pp. 7–10.

LYND, R. and LYND, H. (1929) *Middletown*, New York, Harcourt Brace.

LYND, R. and LYND, H. (1937) *Middletown in Transition*, New York, Harcourt Brace.

MACCOBY, MICHAEL, (1976) *The Gamesman: The New Corporate Leaders*, New York, Simon and Schuster.

MARTINEAU, HARRIET, (1937) *Society in America*, Vol. 3, London, Saunders and Otley, in RAPSON, R. (ed.) (1967) pp. 19–24 (see entry).

MCALLISTER, BERNICE J.S. (1967) *Educator's Status-Roles, Social Antecedents, and Perceptions Related to a Continuum of Traditional-Emergent Values*. Unpublished Ph.D. dissertation, Stanford University.

MEAD, MARGARET, (1943) *And Keep Your Powder Dry*. New York, Morrow.

MERELMAN, RICHARD, (1983) *Making Something of Ourselves*, Berkeley, CA, University of California.

MOFFAT, MICHAEL, (1989) *Coming of Age in New Jersey: College and American Culture*, New Brunswick and London, Rutgers University Press.

NASH, RODERICK, (1982) *Wilderness and The American Mind* (3rd edition), New Haven, Yale University Press.

NAY, BARBARA, (1974) *American Values: An Anthropological Analysis,* Seniors Honors Thesis, Department of Anthropology, Stanford University.

OGBU, JOHN, V. (1987) 'Variability in Minority Responses to Schooling: Nonimmigrants vs. Immigrants', in SPINDLER, G. and L. (eds), *Interpretive Ethnography of Schooling at Home and Abroad,* Hillsdale, Lawrence Erlbaum.

PARKER, RICHARD, (1972) *The Myth of The Middle Class,* New York, Liverwright.

PARTRIDGE, WILLIAM, (1973) *Hippie Ghetto,* New York, Holt, Rinehart and Winston.

PATTISON, E.M., M.D., (1974) 'Marginal Middle Class: Faith Healing and Glossalalia' in *Religious Movements in Contemporary America,* I. ZARETSKY and M. LEONE (eds), Princeton, New Jersey, Princeton University Press.

PERIN, CONSTANCE, (1977) *Everything in Its Place: Social Order and Land Use in America,* Princeton, NJ, Princeton University Press.

PERIN, C. (1988) *Belonging in America: Reading Between the Lines,* Madison, WI, University of Wisconsin Press.

PESHKIN, ALAN, (1978) *Growing up in America: Schooling and the Survival of the Community,* Chicago, Chicago University Press.

PESHKIN, ALAN, (1990) *The Color of Strangers, The Color of Friends,* Chicago, University of Chicago Press.

PILCHER, WILLIAM, W. (1972) *The Portland Longshoremen: A Dispersed Urban Community,* New York, Holt, Rinehart and Winston.

POTTER, DAVID, (1954) *People of Plenty,* Chicago, IL, University of Chicago Press.

POTTER, DAVID, (1964) 'American Women and the American Character', in *American Character and Culture: Some Twentieth Century Perspectives,* J. A. HAGUE, (ed.) Deland, FL., Everett/Edwards, (reprinted in 1979 by Greenwood Press).

POWDERMAKER, HORTENSE, (1950) *Hollywood: The Dream Factory,* Boston: Heath.

RAPSON, R. (ed.) (1967) *Individualism and Conformity in the American Character,* Boston, MA, Heath.

RIESMAN, DAVID, DENNY, R. and GLAZER, N. (1950) *The Lonely Crowd: A Study of the changing American Character,* New Haven, CT, Yale University Press.

RUESCH, J. and BATESON, G. (1951) *Communication: The Social Matrix of Psychiatry,* New York, Mouton.

SANO, TOSHIYUKI, (1989) *Caring Americans: An Ethnography of Riverfront, A Middle-sized Town in the Midwest.* Ph.D. dissertation, Stanford University.

SCHNEIDER, DAVID, (1977) 'Kinship, community and locality in American culture', in *Kin and Communities,* A. LICHTMAN, J. CHALLINOR, (eds) Washington D.C., Smithsonian Institution Press, pp. 155–74.

SHORTRIDGE, JAMES R, (1989) *The Middle West: Its Meaning in American Culture,* Lawrence, Kansas, University Press of Kansas.

SIMONSON, RICK and WALKER, SCOTT (1988) *Multicultural Literacy: Opening The American Mind,* Saint Paul, Minnesota, Graywolf Press.

SPINDLER, GEORGE, (1948) 'American Character as Revealed by the Military', *Psychiatry: Journal for the Operational Statement of Interpersonal Relations*, **11**, pp. 275–81.

SPINDLER, GEORGE D. (1955a) *Sociocultural and Psychological Process in Menomini Acculturation*, University of California Publications in Culture and Society. Vol. 5. Berkeley, CA., University of California Press.

SPINDLER, GEORGE D. (1955b) 'Education in a Transforming American Culture'. *Harvard Educational Review*, **25**, pp. 145–56.

SPINDLER, GEORGE D. (1959) *The Transmission of American Culture*, The Third Burton Lecture, School of Education, Harvard University, Cambridge, MA., Harvard University Press.

SPINDLER, GEORGE D. (1977) 'Change and Continuity in American Core Cultural Values: An Anthropological Perspective'. in *We The People: American Character and Social Change*, G. DiRENZO (Ed.) Westport, CT, Greenwood, pp. 20–40.

SPINDLER, GEORGE D. (1987) 'The Transmission of Culture', in G. SPINDLER, (ed.) *Education and Cultural Process: Anthropological Approaches*, 2nd edition. Prospect HTS, Ill. Waveland Press.

SPINDLER, GEORGE and LOUISE, (1971) 'Fieldwork with the Menominee', in *Being an Anthropologist: Fieldwork in Eleven Cultures*, G. SPINDLER (ed.) New York, Holt, Rinehart and Winston. (Reprinted with new preface, 1987, Prospect HTS, Ill. Waveland Press).

SPINDLER, GEORGE and LOUISE, (1978) 'Identity, Militancy, and Cultural Congruence: The Menominee and Kanai', *The Annals of the American Academy of Political and Social Science*, **436**, pp. 74–85.

SPINDLER, GEORGE and LOUISE, (1983) 'Anthropologists View American Culture'. *Annual Review of Anthropology*. Bernard Siegel, *et al.* (eds.) **12**, pp. 49–78. Palo Alto, CA, Annual Review, Inc.

SPINDLER, GEORGE and LOUISE, (1984) *Dreamers with Power: The Menominee Indians*, Prospect Heights, Ill., Waveland Press, (First ed, 1971), New York, Holt, Rinehart and Winston.

SPINDLER, GEORGE and LOUISE, (1987a) 'Schöenhausen Revisited and the Rediscovery of Culture', in G. and L. SPINDLER, (eds.) *Interpretive Ethnography of Education*. Hilldale, New Jersey, Lawrence Erlbaum Assoc.

SPINDLER, GEORGE and LOUISE, (1987b) 'Cultural Dialogue and Schooling in Schöenhausen and Roseville: A comparative analysis', *Anthropology and Education Quarterly*, **18**: pp. 3–16.

SPINDLER, GEORGE and LOUISE, (1989) 'Instrumental competence, Self-Efficacy, Linguistic Minorities, and Cultural Therapy', *Anthropology and Education Quarterly*, **20**, pp. 36–50.

STEELE, EDWARD D. (1957) 'The Rhetorical Use of the "American Value System" in the 1952 Presidential Campaign Addresses', Unpublished Ph.D. dissertation, Stanford University.

SUAREZ-OROSCO, MARCELO, M. (1989) *Central American Refugees and U.S. Highschools*, Stanford, CA, Stanford University Press.

TAUXE, CAROLINE, (1988) *Family Farmers in an Industrializing County in Western North Dakota,* Ph.D. dissertation, Berkeley, University of California.

TOFFLER, ALVIN, (1970) *Future Shock,* New York, Random House.

TRUEBA, HENRY, SPINDLER, GEORGE, and SPINDLER, LOUISE, (eds), (1989) *What Do Anthropologists Have to Say About Dropouts?* The First Centennial Conference on Children at Risk, School of Education, Stanford University, Basingstoke, Falmer Press.

TURNER, F.J. (1921) *The Frontier in American History,* New York, Holt, Rinehart and Winston in RAPSON, R. (ed.) (1967) pp. 25–27 (see entry).

VARENNE, HENRI, (1977) *Americans Together: Structured Diversity in a Midwestern Town,* New York, Teachers College Press.

VARENNE, HERVE, (1986) *Symbolizing America,* Lincoln, NB., University of Nebraska Press.

VIDICH, ARTHUR J. and BENMAN, J. (1958) *Small Town in a Mass Society,* Princeton, Princeton University Press, (Anchor Books edition 1960).

VOGT, EVON Z. and ALBERT, ETHEL, (eds), (1966) *People of Rimrock: A Study of Values of Five Cultures,* Cambridge, MA, Harvard University Press, (First Athenum edition 1970).

WARNER, W. LLOYD, (1941) *The Social Life of a Modern Community,* Yankee City Series. New Haven, Yale University Press.

WARNER, W. (1953) *American Life: Dream and Reality,* Chicago, University of Chicago Press (Phoenix edition 1962).

WATERS, LOUISE B. (1976) *The Ethnicity of White 'Non-Ethnics',* Unpublished paper.

WEST, J. (1945) *Plainville: USA,* New York, Columbia University Press.

Demographic Sources

CALIFORNIA DEPARTMENT OF FINANCE, (1983) *Population Projections for California Counties: 1980–2020, with age and sex distribution,* Sacramento, CA.

CALIFORNIA DEPARTMENT OF FINANCE, (1988) *Projected Total of California by Race/Ethnicity, July 1, 1970 to July 1, 2020,* Sacramento, CA.

US BUREAU OF CENSUS SERVICE P-23 no. 49, (1970) *Current Population Reports: Special Studies. Population of the United States. Trends and Prospects,* Washington, DC, US Government Printing Office.

US BUREAU OF THE CENSUS, (1981) *Statistical Abstract of the United States* (102nd ed.), Washington, DC, United States Department of Commerce, Bureau of the Census.

US BUREAU OF THE CENSUS, (1987) *Statistical Abstract of the United States* (107th ed.), Washington, DC, US Department of Commerce, Bureau of the Census.

US BUREAU OF THE CENSUS, (1988) *Statistical Abstract of the United States* (108th ed.), Washington, DC, US Department of Commerce, Bureau of the Census.

US DEPARTMENT OF COMMERCE, (1980) *Population Profile of the United States,* Series P-20. No.363. Washington, DC, Bureau of the Census.

Films

ADAIR, PETER, (1976), *Holy Ghost People,* Producer Blair Boyd, Thistle Films, Paduka, Kentucky.

Future Shock (1972), Produced and directed by Alex Grasshoff and narrated by Orson Welles, Carlsbad, CA, CRM Films. (After the book *Future Shock*) ALVIN TOFFLER (1970), New York, Random House.

Index